Ancient Signposts
By Arthur D. Faram

Cover

Signard Stefanson Map of 1550

Dedication

Dedicated to all the nurturing women in the
World, from which men draw their strength.

Second Edition

© *2011*

Introduction

Where do you begin the task of presenting 10,000 years of history, some of it lost in the cavernous wasteland of time, and present it in such a fashion that it touches the uninformed, informs the curious, and converts the misinformed?

This book, *"Ancient Signposts, Messages From Our Ancient Past"*, covers the evolution of civilizations from before Egyptian times to the colonization of the Americas. During the Author's research on Ancient Civilizations it was discovered that down through time an ancient group secretly passed down a legacy of geoglyphs on the shores and highlands of land masses around the world. A well known example of this are the Nazca Lines in Peru. The reason the Nazca lines and other geoglyphs were not discovered until recently is that they are too large to be seen from the ground. And so it is with most geoglyphs. Extensive research on these geoglyphs, which exist on every continent and many islands around the world, have shown that, no matter when or where they were constructed, they all tie into a worldwide network of lines that form a grid connecting the majority of geoglyphs around world. These geoglyphs range in age from the 10,000 year old Yonaguni Pyramid in Japan, to the 250 year old streets of Washington, DC. The book will be of interest to anyone that is interested in knowing the true story about the evolution of a special group of people that have shaped the history of the world. The adventure in which you are about to engage will amaze you, entertain you, surprise you, and, if you have an open mind, will convey information which has heretofore been restricted to speculation. It is no easy task to change the centuries of misinformation, thrown at the citizens of the world, disguised as history. There are many reasons for this deception, but history is forever and should to be recorded faithfully. You will see, in the sign posts left by the ancients, lies a true recording of the evolution of civilizations over many millennia.

During the time that the information for this book was being collected the research of ancient history has progressed exponentially. On a weekly basis there is a newspaper or periodical article about another ancient structure or civilization being discovered somewhere in the world. Just a few decades ago there was no idea that civilized man had existed for so long. So, as you read this material please use your own reasoning to determine whether something is true. Although references will be given here, when available, it is hoped that the reader will place little faith in anyone's information unless there is cooperating proof provided showing that the information is true. Obviously this would place suspicion on most ancient history, which we have to take at face value unless proved incorrect by more compelling evidence. As you read this book you will see history unfolding before your eyes. Many times it will not go in the direction in which we have been taught that it should go. In response to that we should ask ourselves; how much proof was provided to confirm the information which was given to us previously? Most likely we took the information at face value because it was the only information available. Here the reader will be provided with as much cooperating proof of the information presented as practically possible. Much information will be validated by physical evidence, some will be proven with hard facts, and other information can be verified by the flow of historical facts surrounding it. In this manner it is hoped that the reader will come to trust the information presented.

Once the historical background information is presented attention will be focused on physical evidence which will validate or invalidate many historical events. Some of the evidence will have been unknown until now. Other evidence may have been recorded incorrectly due to primitive collection and verification methods. You will be the judge. Evidence will be presented revealing the origin of the Egyptian, Mayan, and Chinese Pyramids, showing how they are related. For the first time you will learn the truth about the colonization of the Americas, the meaning of mysterious Nazca Lines in Peru and a 10,000 year old plan to colonize North America. You will learn that many tribes recorded as American Indians were in fact assimilated from continents other than Asia. You will learn that a land claim on North America occurred thousands of years before Columbus. The reader may be shocked to learn that South America was mapped and colonized over 10,000 years ago.

History is constantly evolving as we discover new facts. The information which you hold in your hands is an attempt to correct a small portion of that history while providing new and revealing historical facts supported by physical evidence.

Arthur D. Faram

Contents

Introduction

Is recorded history all that it seems to be?

Chapter 1. - Geoglyphs ……………………………………..….…………….. 7

How Geoglyphs tell the story of the ancient world?

Chapter 2. - The Secrets of Caral Peru …………………………………………14

The hidden secrets of the oldest city in South America and the key to a 10,000 year old South American land claim.

Chapter 3. - Egypt and the Pyramids …………………………………..… 43

The overlooked secrets of the Egyptian Pyramids; they are more than tombs and astrological observatories

Chapter 4. - The Pyramids of China ………….. 77

Evidence will be presented to show that these pyramids were constructed by the same culture that built the Egyptian and Mayan Pyramids.

Chapter 5. - The Pyramids of Mexico ………………………………….... 83

Evidence that Mesoamerica was planned as part of what is now the United States.

Chapter 6. - The Vikings …………………………………………….... 96

Viking origins and later migration.

Chapter 7. - The Vikings in America ………………………………… 109

Proof that North America was settled long before Columbus.

Chapter 8. - The Mississippians **126**

An indigenous group of Native Americans that show undeniable contact with Europeans between 800 and 1500 AD.

Chapter 9. - The Juan de la Cosa Map of 1500 AD **147**

A stolen map gives up the secrets of Pre-Columbian Exploration of North and South America.

Chapter 10. - The Newport, Rhode Island Tower and the Kensington, Minnesota Runestone **157**

Centuries of mystery surrounding these two enigmas is solved. The keys to a North American land claim.

Chapter 11. – Portuguese History **217**

The key to why North America has denied Portugal's part in the discovery of the New World and why known geoglyphs pointing to Portugal were destroyed.

Chapter 12. - The Diego Rivera Murals of Mexico City **232**

The secrets hidden in Diego's murals that prove that there was an organized plan to unite the world prior to 10,000 BC.

Chapter 13. - The Nazca Lines **244**

The demystifying of the Nazca mystery.

Chapter 14. - Hernando Cortes, The Game Changer **256**

How the invasion of Mexico by Spain's Hernando Cortes begins a reign of Spanish conquest in the Americas that almost cost the future United States their country.

Appendices .... **270 - 290**

Sources .... **291 – 296**

Chapter 1

Geoglyphs

Geoglyphology

This is a story so unbelievable, and so well documented, that it will leave you breathless. But before we begin it is necessary that the reader understand the evolving science of Geoglyphology and how that field, and the associated symbols, relate to this book.

Over the past several years The Faram Foundation has been involved in the research and development of a new and emerging science. That science has been named Geoglyphology. You will realize, as you read through the book, that this science has the ability to rewrite history, as we know it.

During our research it was discovered that down through time civilizations have secretly passed down a legacy of geoglyphs on the shores and highlands of land masses around the world. A well known example of this is the Nazca Lines in Peru. The reason the Nazca lines and other Geoglyphs were not discovered until recently is that they are too large to be seen from the ground. And so it is with most geoglyphs.

The primary validation of the arguments in this book are verified by researched, documented and dated monuments around the world that have existed for millennia. Scholars have discussed and speculated about many of these monuments for centuries, their true purpose having never been discovered. Much of the data in this book are validated by documented and researched monoliths located around the world. Also included are heretofore undiscovered geoglyphs that are now documented in this book. These geoglyphs serve as historical signposts which document and date ancient peoples, their descendents, and their movements around the globe.

Until now the majority of the information available to the Archeologist is gleaned from the information recovered at the dig site. We have discovered that a great majority of the ancient architectural, monolithic and geoglyphic structures built around the world had something in common. That commonality is that the structures were aligned in such a manner that the study of their linear alignment unveils a much larger story and immensely expands the data available for study.

Extensive research on these geoglyphs, which exist on every continent and many islands around the world, have shown that, no matter when or where they were constructed, they all tie into a worldwide network of civilizations that have progressed, prospered and suffered setbacks for millennia. These geoglyphs range in age from the 10,000 year old Yonaguni Pyramid in Japan, to the 250 year old streets of Washington, DC USA.

Data recovered from these studies includes obtaining the geographical range of the culture being studied, the level of sophistication that existed in relation to their understanding of mathematics and geometry, their knowledge of world geography, the discovery of other archeological sites that were unknown prior to the studies, and the dating of the culture itself by the data collected at the offsite locations and the sophistication of the geoglyphs identified at the dig site.

Geoglyphology exists to assist in identifying any collateral data related to a geoglyph that might assist in understanding the culture, or in expanding the search area. By analyzing this newly discovered data a true understanding of our past will emerge. This science also unlocks the pages of history so that the citizens of the world can obtain a true, validated, glimpse into the past.

Glyphs and Geoglyphs

Glyph - A glyph can be any design that is used to convey a message.
Geoglyph - A geoglyph is a glyph that occurs on the ground.
Bearing - A bearing refers to the direction, as determined from a magnetic compass, that any line formed by a geoglyph points in relation to "True North". True North is used because as soon as you begin tracing a magnetic line away from the source, magnetic deviation becomes a factor. Magnetic Deviation exists all over the world and renders magnetic headings useless over long distances because of the error it causes in a magnetic bearing. True headings are derived from Celestial Navigation, GPS, and computer software. These methods produce True Headings which are not distorted by Magnetic Deviation. True bearings, which we will call radials, will be used throughout this book.

Radials - Radials are bearings, converted to a True Course, after they leave the source. At the source Bearings (Magnetic North) and Radials (True North) are the same because no distortion has taken place by moving away from the source. Once a direction away from the source is plotted it must be plotted on a true course, not a magnetic course, in order to avoid magnetic deviation.

Geoglyphs, for the most part, are so large that they can only be recognized from the air. The civilizations that placed these signposts either had the capability of flight, or had an advanced knowledge of mathematics or astronomy well beyond anything we could have imagined for the time. I have visited some sites on the ground and even knowing they are there I find them difficult to locate. The glyphs take on several forms. Some take the form of a triangle, another might be one or more circles, and another may be one or more lines touching or crossing each other. No matter what shape a glyph takes, any line can be a pointer to a place important to the creator of that glyph. The following Plate shows a few examples of how bearings are derived from geoglyphs.

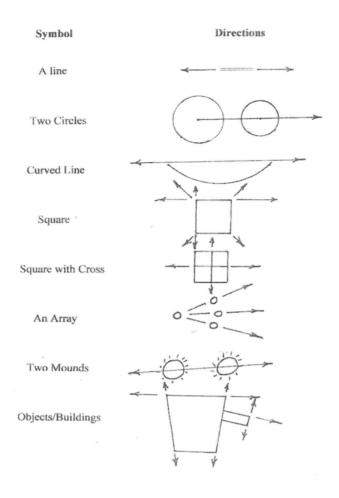

Symbol	Directions

A line

Two Circles

Curved Line

Square

Square with Cross

An Array

Two Mounds

Objects/Buildings

Above are a few examples of radials generated by various angles which may comprise a geoglyph.

After some study it was discovered that many types of construction material were used to construct geoglyphs. These included the arrangement of stones, the planting of different colors of flora, and the sterilizing of the ground, the scraping of the earth to reveal a different color underneath (Nazca), the changing of natural geological features with the features modified or supplemented, the wall alignment of structures (Caral), the alignment of Monoliths (Stonehenge), the alignment of Pyramids (Worldwide), the creation of stone and earth mounds, and more. For instance, the geometry included in the building of the Mississippian Indian mounds, in the Central United States, have proven to be geoglyphic pointers.

Ancient archeological locations, many previously unknown, were identified through Geoglyphology. The accuracy of the calculations of the ancient peoples is incredible. The GPS accuracy of the software program is seldom more accurate than the orientations of the ancient geoglyphs. By calculating the bearing at the source one can follow the extended radial for sometimes thousands of miles and locate a related glyph with little or no error.

The percentage of success in locating a verifiable glyph or ancient location using each of the extended radials of any one glyph was variable, but ran in the range of 75% to 100%. Much of the lack of success was attributed to urbanization, overgrowth, vandalism, etc.. Surprisingly, based on the glyphs that were found, there seems to be an incredible amount of durability built into the geoglyphs. It appears that the meteorological conditions at any given site were considered in determining the materials used. At sites where rain and wind are seldom seen, most glyphs were made of earth. At locations that encountered rain and wind, stones and rock were used. On some geoglyphs, vegetation of contrasting colors were used in order to accent the geoglyph.

Research results indicate that Geoglyphology holds great promise in expanding our understanding of the civilizations that have preceeded us. Through the tireless efforts of many devoted archaeologists, and new methods of discovery, the world is on the cusp of a new awakening. To some this paradigm change will be quite uncomfortable. During any changes, to our current perceptions, it is suggested that we look to the benefits rather than retreating from the changes. Let us embrace the changes as a window to greater understanding and opportunities rather than a threat to the protocols of the past.

SOME GEOGLYPH EXAMPLES

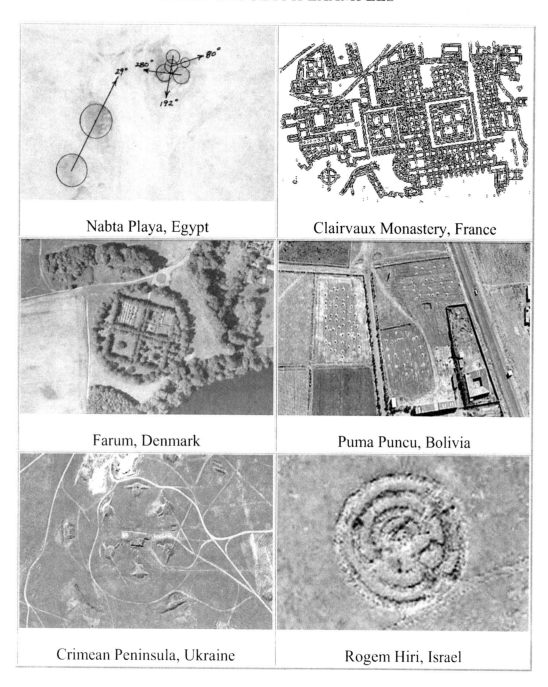

Nabta Playa, Egypt

Clairvaux Monastery, France

Farum, Denmark

Puma Puncu, Bolivia

Crimean Peninsula, Ukraine

Rogem Hiri, Israel

END CHAPTER

Chapter 2

Caral, Peru

A Geoglyphic Study of Caral Peru
Faram Research Foundation - Arlington, Texas

The function of Geoglyphology, as it relates to Archaeology, is to expand both the search area and the knowledge base available to the Archaeologist.

Until now the majority of the information available to the Archeologist is gleaned from the information recovered at the dig site. In recent years it has been discovered that a great majority of the ancient architectural, monolithic and geoglyphic structures built around the world have something in common. That commonality is that the structures were aligned in such a manner that the study of their linear alignment unveils a much larger story and immensely expands the data available to the archaeologist and the related disciplines.

Data recovered from sites, that included Geoglyphology in their study, included obtaining the geographical range of the culture being studied. Also obtained were; the level of sophistication that existed in relation to their understanding of mathematics and geometry, their knowledge of world geography, the discovery of other archaeological sites that were unknown prior to the studies, and the dating of the culture itself by the data collected at related offsite locations.

The success of these studies shows that Geoglyphology can play a major role in expanding the knowledge base available to the Archaeologist.

The word Archaeology is derived from the Greek word archaiologia and is the study of past human societies, primarily through the recovery and analysis of the material culture and environmental data which they have left behind, which includes artifacts, architecture, biofacts and cultural landscapes. Archaeology developed out of antiquarianism in Europe during the 19th century, and has since become a discipline practiced across the world.

Archaeology studies human history from the development of the first stone tools in eastern Africa 3.4 million years ago up until recent decades. It is of most importance for learning about prehistoric societies, when there are no written records for historians to study, and which makes up over 99% of total human history, from the Paleolithic until the advent of literacy in any given society. Archaeology has various different goals, which range from studying human evolution to cultural evolution and understanding culture history.

The current archaeological discipline involves surveyance, excavation and eventually analysis of data collected in order to learn more about the past. In broad scope, archaeology relies on cross-disciplinary research. It draws upon anthropology, history, art history, classics, ethnology, geography, geology, linguistics, physics, information sciences, chemistry, statistics, paleoecology, paleontology, paleozoology, paleoethnobotany, and paleobotany.

This study introduces a new tool to the archaeological disciplines referred to as Geoglyphology. A geoglyph is a drawing on the ground, or a large motif, or design produced on the ground, either by arranging stones, stone fragments, gravel or earth to create a positive geoglyph (stone arrangement, wall alignments, petroforms and earth mounds) or by removing darker surface stones to expose a lighter surface underneath. (a negative geoglyph). Recently some geoglyphs have been discovered in the Amazon Rainforest, in Brazil, which led to claims about unknown civilizations that may have inhabited the area in the past.

For centuries the information available to archaeologist has been restricted, mainly, to the information available directly from the dig site. Geoglyphology, which has been tested and proven valid at archaeological sites around the world, will allow the archaeologist to expand their exploration away from the site, sometimes hundreds and even thousands of miles.

This study will focus on the newly discovered complex called Caral in the Supa Valley Peru. Caral is located approximately 85 miles North of Lima. Peru. After carbon Dating, Caral is now being called the oldest city in the Americas (Circa 2700 BC).

Until now the majority of information obtained from the architectural complex at Caral is from objects discovered on site. Although the information gathered from these objects are of immense importance, these discoveries depend on information available from objects discovered at the dig site. Conversely, the absence of certain objects can lead to speculation. That is the case with the Caral complex in that, to date, no pottery or burial sites have been found. The ancient Caral archeological site was chosen for this presentation because it offers one of the best demonstrations of Geoglyphology at work.

Data recovered from the study of the Caral site will include obtaining the geographical range of the culture being studied, learning the level of sophistication that existed in relation to their understanding of mathematics and geometry, exposing their knowledge of geography, identifying other archaeological sites that were unknown prior to the study, and provide other critical information about the culture of the inhabitants existing in the geographical boundaries defined by the geoglyphs.

On 27 April 2001 came the stunning announcement in the journal *Science* that the emergence of urban life and complex agriculture in the New World occurred nearly a millennium earlier than previously believed.

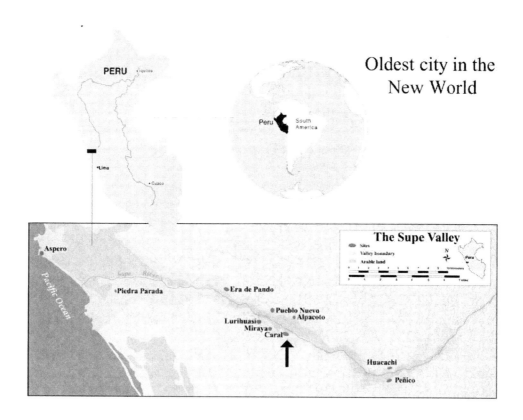

Oldest city in the New World

Map of Central Zone at Caral - Courtesy of the Field Museum

Radiocarbon dates from the ancient city of Caral, (10* 53' 30.72"S - 77* 31' 18.84"W) in the Supe Valley of Peru, 23 km from the coast, show that monumental architecture there was under construction as early as 2627 B.C. until about 2000 B.C., even before ceramics and maize were introduced to the region. (By comparison, the Great Pyramid of Khufu in Egypt was built between 2480 and 2600 B.C.) Also remarkable is the enormous size of the urban complex: 65 hectares in the central zone itself, encompassing six large platform mounds (or "pyramids"), many smaller platform mounds, two sunken circular plazas, and diverse architectural features including residential districts. Caral is by far the largest recorded site in the Andean region with dates older than 2000 B.C. and appears to be the model for the urban design adopted by Andean civilizations that rose and fell over the span of four millennia.

Excavations at Caral have been undertaken by Jonathan Haas from Chicago's Field Museum, Ruth Shady Solis of the Anthropology Museum at the Universidad Nacional Mayor de San Marcos and the Field Museum, and Winifred Creamer, Northern Illinois University and the Field. It was featured in a Science article in April 2001, after a long and careful investigation into the radiocarbon dates from the site.

The interesting thing about Caral and the rest of the Supe Valley sites, is that it illustrates the problems archaeologists have dealing with in so-called "urban settlements" and "state societies." Building monumental architecture such as pyramids and irrigation canals and cities takes sophisticated planning. When archaeologists first came upon the cities of our ancient pasts, we began developing our theories of why states rise. One of the most prevalent theories was that it takes a combination of factors to create the political climate that creates public works; and that usually means full scale agriculture, craft specialization, a writing system, ceramic production, social stratification, even metallurgy.

But the Supe Valley sites, and other early urban settlements such as Catalhoyuk in Turkey [6300-5500 BC], apparently arose without all of these elements. Although we can't know the political structure of the people who built Caral, to date no ceramics, evidence of metallurgy or writing has been found.

Dr. Shelia Pozorski, a professor at the University of Texas-Pan American who with her husband, Tom, has studied other Andean sites for 30 years, said the finding helped overturn what has been known as the maritime hypothesis. This is the idea that complex Andean societies, precursors of the Incas, evolved from the coast, where reliance on fishing required some level of social organization, to inland sites, developing fully only when ceramics appeared around 1800 to 1500 BC.

"It makes it more of a quantum leap, rather than a moderately rapid crawl," Dr. Pozorski said. "Rather than having coastal precursors to inland complexity, the two areas are developing at the same time."

Another expert in Andean anthropology, Dr. Richard L. Burger, director of the Peabody Museum of Natural History at Yale, described the new work as "... the nail in the coffin of the maritime hypothesis."

Dr. Haas said, in his paper on Caral published in the journal *Science*, that before the rise of Caral civilization in the region amounted to a few small coastal villages, with perhaps a hundred people or so in each, and other smaller bands of hunter-gatherers. By 2700 B.C., he said, several larger villages began to appear.

"But then all of a sudden you've got Caral, and probably at least one of its neighbors," Dr. Haas said. "It's bigger by an order of magnitude than anything before." While it is not yet possible to estimate the population of Caral — much more archaeological work remains to be done — Dr. Haas said that the number was in the thousands, not hundreds.

Dr. Haas studied Caral with his wife, Dr. Winifred Creamer, a professor of anthropology at Northern Illinois University, and Dr. Ruth Shady of the Universidad Nacional Mayor de San Marcos in Peru. Their paper dating and describing the site was published in a previous edition of the Science Journal.

Caral was first discovered by archaeologists about 1905, and has been explored only intermittently. Anthropologists have largely ignored Caral, considering it puzzling, Dr. Haas said.

Pottery has never been found at the site, and its absence would ordinarily suggest that the civilization existed before 1800 B.C. But Dr. Haas said that for many experts the sheer size of the place — and the level of societal complexity that it implies — meant that it had to be newer. The consensus, he said, was that "something that big cannot be that early." So the lack of ceramics, by this way of thinking, was only an anomaly. Since those statements the City of Caral has been Carbon Dated to 2627 BC.

The Sacred City of Caral-Supe (Peru), the oldest centre of civilization in the Americas, was inscribed on UNESCO's World Heritage List by the World Heritage Committee, chaired by Maria Jesus San Segundo, the Ambassador and Permanent Delegate of Spain to UNESCO.

In this study you will be exposed to the terms geoglyphs, glyphs, bearings, radials, and survey markers. The following will explain some of the terms used in Geoglyphology.

GLYPH - A glyph can be any design that is used to convey a message.
GEOGLYPH - A geoglyph, as described previously, is a glyph that occurs on the ground.
BEARING - The bearings in this study refer to the direction that any line, formed by a geoglyph, points in relation to "Magnetic North". This is important to understand because as soon as you begin tracing a line away from the source, magnetic deviation becomes a factor. Magnetic Deviation exists all over the world and renders a compass useless over long distances because of the error it causes in a magnetic bearing. Magnetic bearings can be taken at the source of a Geoglyph and are correct at the source. However, in order for the bearing to be correct over any distance one must use a "True Heading", a radial. True headings are derived from Celestial Navigation, GPS, and computer software. These methods only produce True Headings which are not distorted by Magnetic Deviation. The computer software "Google Earth Pro" is the method that was used in this study.
RADIALS - Radials, in this study, refer to the projected "True Heading" after it leaves the origination point.

Geoglyphs, for the most part, are so large that they can only be recognized from the air.[2] The circle glyph depicted in this study, in the center of South America, was located by projecting radials from the glyphs located at the City of Caral. The circle glyph is 22 miles wide. This is most likely why most geoglyphs have not been discovered before now. The Nazca lines are a good example of large geoglyphs. I have visited some sites on the ground and even knowing they are there I find them difficult to locate. The glyphs take on several forms. Some take the form of a triangle, another might be one or more circles, and another may be one or more lines touching or crossing each other. No mater what shape a glyph takes, any line can be a pointer to a place important to the creator of that glyph.

This study was undertaken after the discovery of several Geoglyphs, the likes of which had never before been reported. The only way that this was made possible was by using the flexibility and accuracy available in the "Google Earth Pro" software program. This software program contains a model of the surface of the Earth made from a composite of actual satellite photos. The program has great flexibility and allows for a host of adjustments, depending upon the operators needs. The one most crucial to this study is the ability to draw a line on the face of the Earth while at the same time reading the magnetic bearing from the source and the true heading of the extend radial, without magnetic deviation being a factor. The program also incorporates a zoom feature which allows a close-up view of the Earth's surface as depicted in the photos that follow.

After some study it was discovered that many mediums were used to construct geoglyphs. These included the arrangement of stones, the planting of different colors of flora, and the sterilizing of the ground, the scraping of the earth to reveal a different color underneath (Nazca), the changing of natural geological features with the features modified or supplemented, the wall alignment of structures (Caral), the alignment of Monoliths (Stonehenge), the alignment of Pyramids (Worldwide), the creation of stone and earth mounds, and more. For instance, the mounds of the Mississippian Indians, in the central United States have been proven to be geoglyph pointers.

Curiously most of the geoglyphs point to other geoglyphs somewhere in the world. In this manner the validity of the study was verified as accurate and over three hundred geoglyphs and ancient archeological locations, many previously unknown, were identified. The accuracy of the calculations of the ancient peoples is incredible. The GPS accuracy of the software program is seldom more accurate than the orientations of the ancients. By calculating the bearing at the source one can follow the extended radial for sometimes thousands of miles and locate a related glyph with little or no error. This most likely was accomplished with a sun compass.

The percentage of success in locating a verifiable glyph or ancient location using each of the extended radials of any one glyph was variable, but ran in the range of 75% to 100%. Much of the lack of success was attributed to urbanization, overgrowth, vandalism, etc.. Surprisingly, based on the glyphs that were found, there seems to be an incredible amount of durability built into the geoglyphs. It appears that the meteorological conditions at any given site were considered in determining the materials used. At sites where rain and wind are seldom seen, most glyphs were made of earth. At locations that encountered rain and wind, stones and rock were used.

As stated before, Caral, Peru was chosen as the centerpiece of this study because of two factors. First, it is a new find and still has many mysterious and unknown aspects. Secondly, it is a large complex that offers many Geographilogical aspects. The findings of the Caral study are described below.

The Caral Peru Complex
(10* 53' 30.72"S - 77* 31' 18.84"W)

Caral was inhabited between roughly 2600 BC and 2000 BC, enclosing an area of more than 60 hectors. Caral was described by its excavators as the oldest urban center in the Americas, a claim that was later challenged as other ancient sites were found nearby. Accommodating more than 3,000 inhabitants, it is the best studied and one of the largest Norte Chico sites known.

There are over 19 other pyramid complexes scattered across the 35 square mile (80 km²) area of the Supe Valley. The date of 2627 BCE is based on carbon dating woven reed carrying bags that were found in Situ. These bags were used to carry the stones that were used for the construction of the pyramids. The material is an excellent candidate for dating, thus allowing for a high precision. The site may date even earlier as samples from the oldest parts of the excavation have yet to be dated. The town had a population of approximately 3000 people. But there are 19 other sites in the area, allowing for a possible total population of 20,000 people for the Supe valley. All of these sites in the Supe valley share similarities with Caral. They had small platforms or stone circles. Dr. Shady, of the Museum of Archaeology at the National University of San Marcos, Lima, Peru, believes that Caral was the focus of this civilization, which itself was part of an even vaster complex, trading with the coastal communities and the regions further inland – as far as the Amazon. (Science 27 April 2001: 723-726.)

Dr. Shady's belief in a civilization stretching East to the mouth of the Amazon River is substantiated in this study. Other studies confirm that the civilization, of which Caral was part, used the Amazon river for transportation from it's headwaters to the mouth of the river. Headlines have been appearing recently about geoglyphs being found all through the Amazon Jungle as land is cleared for farming.

The Caral complex was split into the five main sections addressed in the photos below. This was done to allow for close-up photos and a more detailed description. The radials described below the photos are the endpoints for the given radial. A logical question would be to ask; How do you know that these are the true endpoints for the given radials? To answer that fully would require documenting two years of study on the subject. However, I will attempt to provide a short but satisfactory answer. First of all we do not consider a point as an endpoint unless there have been other geoglyphs pointing to that same location. This is not unusual because most of the geoglyphs around the world form a linier network. On occasion, an endpoint will be accepted if the location fits into the apparent theme of the geoglyph.

That leads us to the second reason an endpoint might be accepted. Most geoglyphs follow a pattern. Some geoglyphs will have been made to show seaports that are important to the originator. Other geoglyphs may have been constructed to outline a specific territory that is important to the originator. Some geoglyphs are constructed to verify that another geoglyph was interpreted correctly.

That leads to the third reason endpoints might be accepted independently of other considerations. There may be present some geometric pattern that includes a previously unidentified endpoint. That endpoint may be accepted if it is a part of a geometric pattern that confirms, without question, that the information gathered from the source glyph is valid. It is our experience that the creators of these geoglyphs will present some sign that verifies that the purpose of a geoglyph was solved correctly. In the case of the Caral glyphs that verification is the 360/180 degree line that begins in the center of the meteor crater, as defined by the Antilles Islands, and proceeds South in a line that passes through the circle glyph, identified by the Caral 116 and 117 degree radials, and terminates precisely at the tip of South America. By outlining the crater with the Antilles Islands endpoints the originators demonstrated not only their accuracy but their knowledge of the topography. Another confirmation is the Equilateral Triangle formed by the Galapagos Islands, the center of the Columbian meteor crater, and the man made circle glyph identified by the Caral 116 and 117 degree radials.

The following photo array is a presentation of our findings:

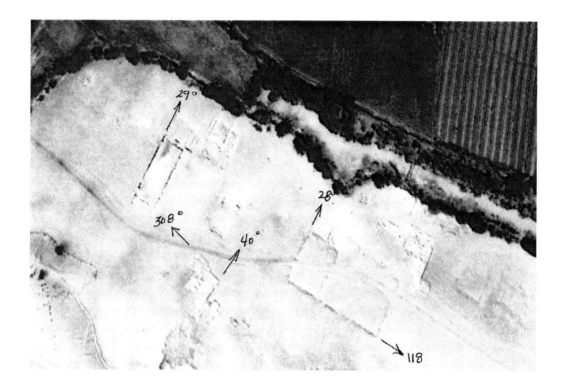

Caral Peru, Plate 1

Endpoints for the bearings displayed in the preceding photo.

028 Degree Radial - Saint Kitts Island, Antilles
029 Degree Radial - Montserrat Island, Antilles
040 Degree Radial - Entrance to Orinoco River, Venezuela
118 Degree Radial - Headwaters of the Amazon
308 Degree Radial - Galapagos Islands

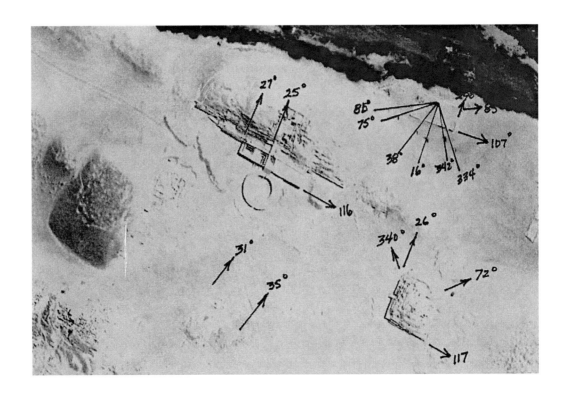

Caral Peru, Plate 2

Endpoints for the bearings displayed in the preceding photo.

016 Degree Radial - Dominican Republic
025 Degree Radial - Roques Island, Venezuela
026 Degree Radial - Anquilla Island, Antilles
027 Degree Radial - Saint Kits Island, Antilles
029 Degree Radial - Montserrat Island, Antilles
031 Degree Radial - Dominica Island, Antilles
035 Degree Radial - Granada Island, Antilles
038 Degree Radial - Trinidad Island, Antilles
072 Degree Radial - Entrance to Amazon River, Brazil
075 Degree Radial - The Ancient Altamera Canals, Amazon, Brazil, (3* 14'
21.74"S - 51* 39' 06.42'W)
085 Degree Radial - East Tip of South America
107 Degree Radial - Largest Open Pit Gold Mine in the World. (13* 00'
36"S - 70* 32' 34"W)

116 Degree Radial - North Rim of Santa Rosa Geoglyph, Bolivia, (17* 10.04' 48"S - 63* 43' 20.57'W)

117 Degree Radial - South Rim of Santa Rosa Geoglyph, Bolivia, (17* 10.04' 48"S - 63* 43' 20.57'W)

334 Degree Radial - Entrance to Gulf of Guayaquil, Ecuador

340 Degree Radial - Chichin Itza, Mexico

342 Degree Radial - Puna Island, Gulf of Guayaquil, Ecuador

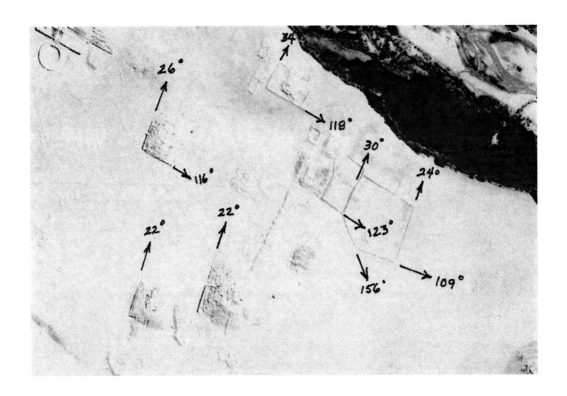

Caral Peru, Plate 3

Endpoints for the bearings displayed in the preceding photo.

022 Degree Radial - East End of Puerto Rico
024 Degree Radial - East End of Virgin Islands, Antilles
026 Degree Radial - Anguilla Island, Antilles
030 Degree Radial - Guadalupe Island, Antilles
034 Degree Radial - Santa Lucia Island, Antilles
109 Degree Radial - Largest Open Pit Gold Mine in The World. (13* 00'
36"S - 70* 32' 34"W)
116 Degree Radial - Machu Pichu
123 Degree Radial - Lake Titicaca, Peru/Bolivia
156 Degree Radial - Bahia Blanca, Argentina with Geoglyphs

Caral Peru, Plate 4

Endpoints for the bearings displayed in the preceding photo.

020 Degree Radial - Puerto Rico

023 Degree Radial - Saint Thomas Island, Antilles

026 Degree Radial - Saint Martin Island, Antilles

031 Degree Radial - Guadalupe Island, Antilles

292 Degree Radial - Reciprocal 112 - 10000 year old mining site called La
Oroya. (11* 31' 25"S - 75* 54' 29"W)

304 Degree Radial - Ancient City of Barranca, Peru, Possibly earlier than
Caral. (10* 44' 35"S - 77* 44' 53")

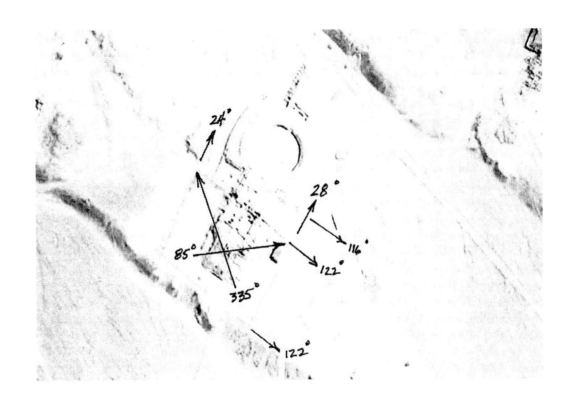

Caral Peru, Plate 5

Endpoints for the bearings displayed in the preceding photo.

024 Degree Radial - East End of Virgin Islands
028 Degree Radial - Saint Kitts Island, Antilles
085 Degree Radial - East Tip of South America
116 Degree Radial - Machu Pichu, Peru
122 Degree Radial - Lake Titicaca, Peru/Bolivia
335 Degree Radial - Entrance to Gulf of Guayaquil, Ecuador. (3* 44' 55"S -
80* 41' 42"W)

The Caral Peru Amphitheater Shown in Plate 5
Graphic by Don Foley

Overshadowed by the dispute over how Caral started is the mystery of why it ended. Archaeologists have found no evidence of an invasion or a rebellion. Instead, city residents systematically covered over plazas, pyramids, and other buildings with gravel and pebbles 3,800 years ago and then left. Their efforts, plus the region's dry climate, helped preserve such buildings as the 36-foot-high Amphitheater Pyramid, which was apparently used for religious functions. A set of 32 flutes was found on the flat area surrounding the circular amphitheater. Other musical instruments, including 37 horns, were found elsewhere in the 130,000-square-foot stone-and-mortar structure. - From the *Discover Science* Website by Kenneth Miller September 2005 issue; published online September 9, 2005.

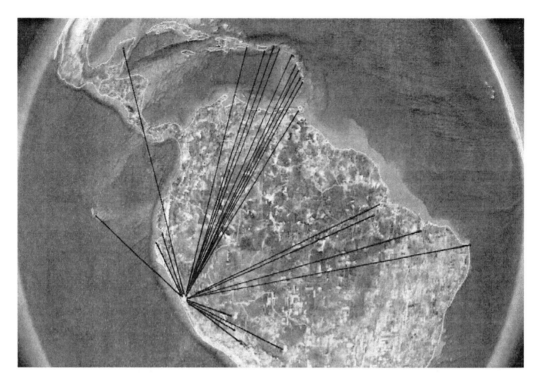

The Radials Defined by the Geoglyphs in the City of Caral

The Santa Rosa Circular Glyph
(17* 10.04' 48"S - 63* 43' 20.57"W)

The Santa Rosa Geoglyph is 22.7 miles across and was defined by the Caral 116 degree radial touching Northeast side and the 117 degree radial touching the Southwest side. The topography of the Glyph does not seem to lend it self to volcanic or meteorite action but appears to be manmade. Farming and the river have divided the glyph on the West side. Therefore part of the glyph is West of the river. This glyph was strategically placed to form the geometric designs that are depicted in the following photos.

The Columbian Triangle, as Outlined by the Endpoints of the Caral Radials.

The triangle is composed of the Galapagos Islands, The Santa Rosa circular Geoglyph, and the center of the Columbian Impact Craters' final resting point. The center of the crater was defined by the Caral radials pointing out the islands forming the half circle around the crater. The vertexes of the triangle form a perfect equilateral triangle.

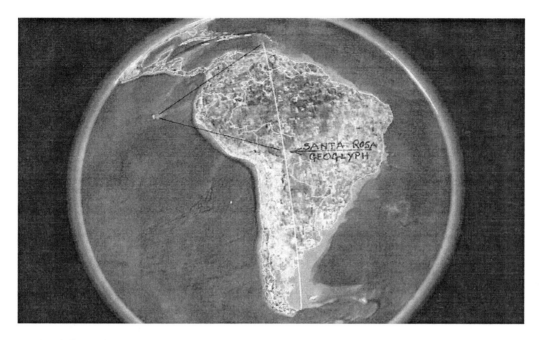

The 360/180 Degree line and Columbian Triangle as they relate to the Santa Rosa Geoglyph.

The Equilateral Triangle and the perfectly placed North/South line that crosses South America is the validation, mentioned previously, that the puzzle was completed as intended by the originator.

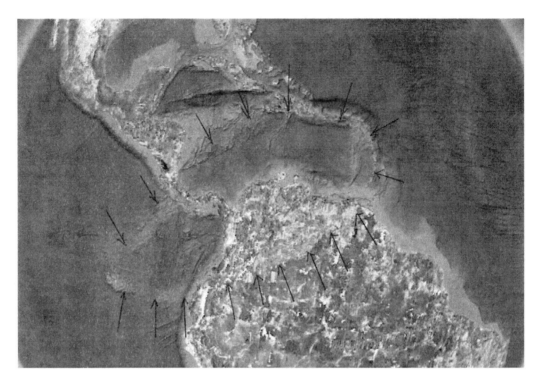

An Outline of the Columbian Crater

The Columbian Crater is defined in the above photo by the arrows that appear around the perimeter. The action of Tectonic plates, which run the length of Mesoamerica, have caused the rift to raise, thereby reconnecting North And South America. This is demonstrated by the different colors of earth that exist along the crater edge.

One of the main advantages of Geoglyphology is the identification of related sites that may have gone unnoticed had Geoglyphology not been used.

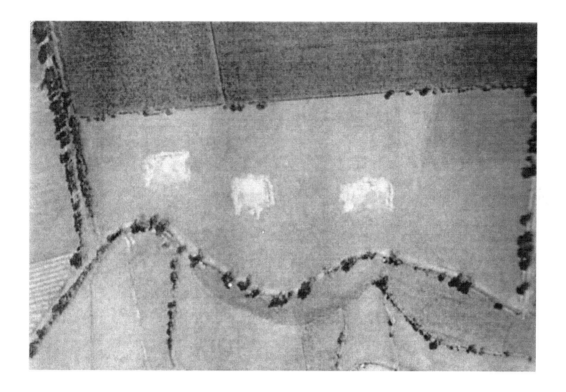

The Ruins at Barranca, Peru
(10* 44' 35"S - 77* 44' 53")

A few of the ruins at the ancient city of Barranca, Peru. This location is identified by the Caral 304 degree radial. This city could be older than Caral by the fact that it is closer to the ocean.

The Ancient Altamera Canals
(3* 14' 21.74"S - 51* 39' 06.42'W)

This geoglyph, identified by the Caral 075 degree radial, is actually a series of man made canals designed in the shape of a star. The glyph mirrors the territory depicted in the Caral Geoglyph which would tend to place it in the same time period of habitation.

Endpoints for the bearings displayed in the above photo.

033 Degree Radial - Isla Mexiana, Brazil. Entrance to the Amazon River
059 Degree Radial - Belem, Brazil. Entrance to Bay of Maraho, Brazil
087 Degree Radial - Bay of Sao Marcos, Sao Luis, Brazil
188 Degree Radial - Montevideo, Rio de la Plata, Uruguay
195 Degree Radial - Southern Tip of South America
295 Degree Radial - Shortest Way Across Panama
298 Degree Radial - Mexico City
324 Degree Radial - Trinidad Island, Venezuela

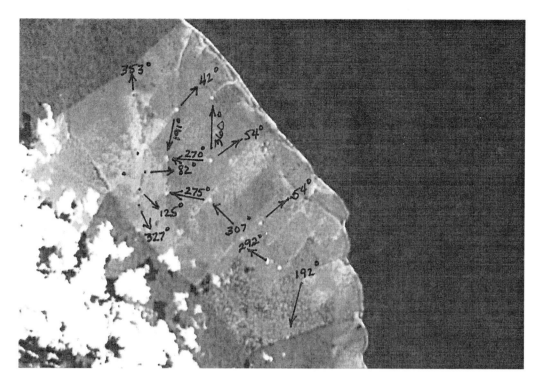

The Altamera Dot Glyphs
(2* 32' 26.71"S - 52* 03' 53.65"W)

This glyph is a few miles north of the Altamera Canal glyphs and West of
the mouth of the Amazon River. The glyph is most likely of later origin.
First, it is comprised of light colored objects and lines placed in a strategic
order on the ground. Secondly, it speaks of places not mentioned in the Caral
and Altamesa glyphs. By the time this glyph was made the originators were
aware of the African Continent.

Endpoints for the bearings displayed in the above photo.

042 Degree Radial - Isla de Mexiana, Entrance to Amazon River, Brazil
054 Degree Radial - Cape Verde Islands, West Africa
093 Degree Radial - Bahia de Sao Marcos, Sao Luis, Brazil
125 Degree Radial - South Tip of Africa
191 Degree Radial - Southern Tip of South America
192 Degree Radial - Beginning of the Antarctic Meteor Trench. (41* 48'

10'S - 47* 07" 44"W) The importance of this point is discussed in a later paper.

262 Degree Radial - Western Most Point in South America
270 Degree Radial - Orientation Radial 270/090
275 Degree Radial - Where the Equator and the Shore of Ecuador Meet
292 Degree Radial - Shortest way Across Panama
307 Degree Radial - Eastern Tip of Yucatan, Mexico
327 Degree Radial - Georgetown, Guyana
353 Degree Radial - Reciprocal 173 - Southern Tip of South America

Chavín de Huantár
(09* 30' 10.23S - 78* 13' 21.78W)

The Chavin de Huantar site exists 113 miles North of Caral. Before the discovery of Caral this city was once considered the oldest city in the Americas. This photo is presented to demonstrate the similarities in the two sites. However, the Chavin site uses a combination of non parallel architectural lines as well as glyph lines on the ground. These lines tell a story just as the Caral lines did.

The following statement, taken from the description of Caral in *Wikipedia*, fully illustrates why the use of Geoglyphology would benefit the field of Archeology. *"Paul Kosok discovered Caral (Chupacigarro Grande) in 1948, but it received little attention until recently because it appeared to lack many typical artifacts that were sought at archeological sites throughout the Andes at the time."* The use of Geoglyphology, had it been available in 1948, would have given Dr. Kosok other avenues to explore which were directly related to the newly discovered site.

Irena Nazarova, a world renowned writer on Archeological sites, states that near Caral a geoglyph of 48 by 26 meters was found depicting a profile facing the west. It is thought to be used for astronomic calculations, weather and natural phenomena forecasts.

All these findings confirm the high level of scientific, astronomic, technological knowledge, culture and art of the ancient civilization of Caral. We cannot help but mention one of the recent hypotheses: Caral was also a cradle of quechua – one of the most widespread languages on the continent. The new theory contradicts the generally accepted version about appearance of quechua in the Andes, but it has a lot of supporters.

Today we can be absolutely sure to say that Caral was used as a model for future civilizations (which was revealed in the culture of Chavin). Study of the past of Caral will force many to review their theories and rewrite many history textbooks.

The results of this study reveal the following:

Geoglyphs have been incorporated into the architecture of the Caral complex.

Geoglyphs can hasten and enhance the discovery of critical information available to the Scientist about a newly discovered site.

Geoglyphs can indicate at least the minimum range of the geographic dispersement of a civilization.

Geoglyphs can uncover a hidden sophistication in a society which may have gone unnoticed from data gathered at a dig site.

Geoglyphs can reveal other sites, related to the initially discovered site, which may have never been discovered.

Geoglyphs may provide critical information about a society that was not available at the originally discovered location.

END CHAPTER

Chapter 3

Egypt and The Pyramids

EGYPT

Egypt displays the same geometric knowledge and territorial definition in the building of the Pyramids as did Caral Peru and other Egyptian Monoliths. One of the monoliths constructed, after Caral, and prior to the Pyramids at Giza, was the recently discovered complex at Nabta Playa. Nabta Playa contains some of the most interesting relics yet found in Egypt. These are relics that are quite different from the Northern Egyptian relics normally seen in museums around the world. The archaeologists on this site are not ready to reveal this to the public, and therefore a vail of secrecy surrounds this dig. At the time the pyramids were built, there were two religious factions living in Egypt. There were the Northern Egyptians, of which most people are familiar, with there art, lavish lifestyle, and many Gods. There were also the Southern Egyptians living in the Southern Nile Valley who worshiped only one God and had a great influence on a later religion called Christianity. The Southern Nile Egyptians are the group which will be addressed in this book. Most people do not know that Southern Egypt has a Christian Church built in 43AD and that the majority of Egypt was Christian until the Muslim invasion circa 700AD.

A Model of the Nabta Playa Stone Geoglyph - Circa 7000AD

Nabta Playa is an internally drained basin that served as an important ceremonial center for nomadic tribes during the early part of the Holocene epoch. Located 100 km west of Abu Simbel in southern Egypt, Nabta contains a number of standing and toppled megaliths. They include flat, tomb-like stone structures, and a small stone circle that predates Stonehenge and other similar prehistoric sites by at least 1000 years.

The site was first discovered in 1974 by a group of scientists headed by Fred Wendorf, an Anthropology Professor from Southern Methodist University in Texas. The team had stopped for a break from their uncomfortable drive from the Libyan border to the Nile Valley when, as Wendorf stated, "We were standing there minding our own business, when we noticed potsherds and other artifacts." Throughout the 1970's and 1980's, Wendorf returned to Nabta several times. "We determined that humans had occupied the Nabta area off and on for thousands of years, dating from as early as 11,000 years ago up until about 4,800 years ago." The disappearance of the inhabitants from Nabta Playa coincides almost exactly with the building of Stonehenge in Britain. Although Nabta Playa was occupied for more then 5,000 years, the majority of the stone structures and other artifacts originated between 7,000 and 6,500 years ago. This era was considered by most to be the height of human occupation at Nabta. It is also the period in which Woodhenge was built in southern Britain. A study is pending that will compare the pottery shards from the Woodhenge and Stonehenge sites with the pottery shards at Nabta Playa to determine if there is a connection. The general consensus is that the location was abandoned when the Nile River, whose old course was once near Nabta Playa, begin migrating East to its present location.

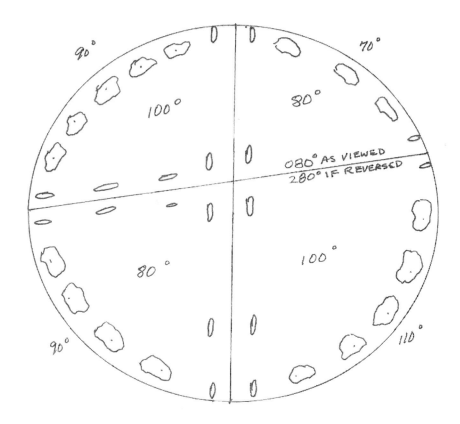

A Drawing of the Nabta Playa Stone Circle as seen from above

One of the few secrets of Nabta Playa that the public has been allowed to see, is the stone megalith depicted above. The drawing is of the Nabta Playa Circle is as it would appear from above. The degrees depicted on the inside of the circle are the degrees formed by the intersecting lines. The degrees measured from the center of the circle appear on the outside of the circle. This oddity occurs because the two lines do not intersect in the center of the circle. The East West line appears to be in a 080/260 degree orientation. We therefore did the usual tracking of the two bearings to see if they intersected any known or interesting points. They did not cross any points of significance. It was then that I realized that on the left side of the circle there were three numbers screaming to be noticed, all of 90 degrees. Knowing that all ancient maps are oriented in the 090 degree direction I flipped the circle over. Now instead of adding 80 degrees to North we subtracted 80 degrees from North. The resulting bearing was 280 degrees. We then begin tracking the 280 degree radial to see where it might go. We hit the jackpot. On the West coast of Africa was spotted a group of geoglyphs at the Gulfo de Cintra. We learned after plotting the geoglyph, That the glyph was associated with both Nabta Playa, the future location of the Pyramid at Giza, and locations around the rim of the Atlantic Ocean which would play an important part in world history later in time. (See the following plates.)

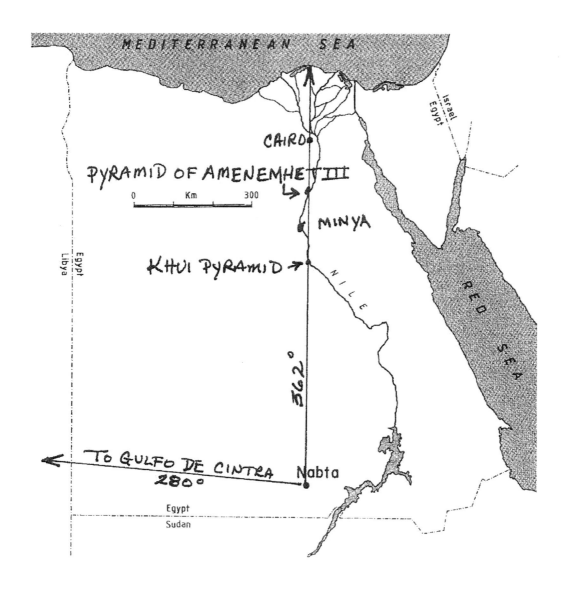

The Nabta Playa location in Egypt

Nabta Playa is located on the East West line of the Summer Solstice as it existed in 7000 BC. The 362 degree radial from the Nabta Playa Circle, passes through the Khui Pyramid on the Nile at Beni Sharan, Egypt. The Khui Pyramid is in the Nile valley near many Coptic Christian settlements and monuments. The 002 degree bearing from Nabta Playa also passes through the Pyramid of King Amenemhet III and continues on to pass through the City of Cairo, the location of Giza Pyramid. The Khui and

Amenemhet Pyramids lie North and South of the ancient city of Minya, Egypt. Interestingly enough, Minya is the birthplace of King Khufu, the builder of the Giza pyramid in Cairo, the largest of the pyramids. It would be difficult to think that the orientation of the North/South radial of the Nabta Plays circle is a coincidence, especially when the orientation of the East/West radial is considered.

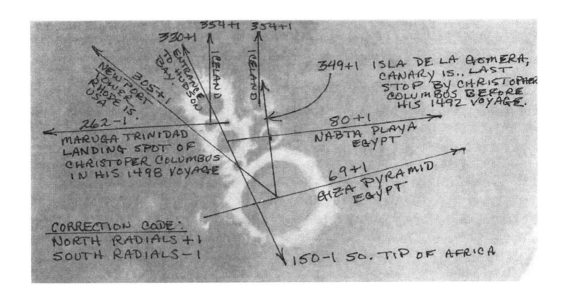

Gulfo de Cintra Glyphs, Western Sahara, Africa

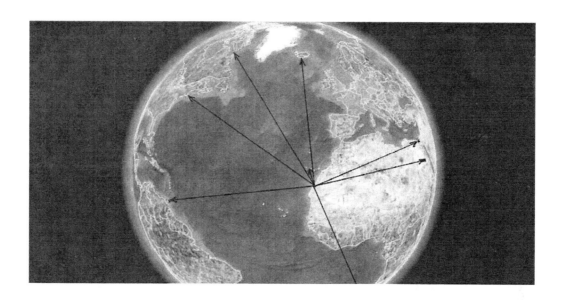

Gulfo de Cintra Radials, Western Sahara, Africa

The glyphs at Gulfo de Cintra, Sahara, West Africa, are some of the most spectacular that we have encountered in all our investigations around the world. First, the geoglyphs are very clear, which leaves is no doubt where the centers of the defining circles are. This is due to the fact that there is very little erosion in the area. Secondly, all the resulting radials point to well established geoglyphic markers that leave no doubt as to where they were intended to point. Thirdly, the glyph is obviously tied to both the Nabta Playa Circle and the Giza Pyramid location because their configurations are mutually supporting. Fourth, and possibly most important, the circles don't appear to have been formed by conventional human methods of the day, as with other glyphs. If this is true then it raises the old chicken and the egg question. Was there a meteor strike that formed a random pattern from which the Egyptians adjusted their agenda to match the pattern, or did an intelligent life force cause the meteors to fall in a pattern that fit an existing plan? Not having visited the site I cannot yet answer the question as to how the glyphs were made. I can only say that they appear as meteor strikes. As you will see at the end of this chapter, there exists another important site, formed by meteors, where the impressions are so large that they could not have been man made. However, the question still lingers, did the ancients adapt their beliefs to the meteor strikes or were the meteor strikes sent by an intelligent life force to fit a situation? One thing is sure, it proves that either an ancient intelligent life form existed that was able to hurl giant objects with extreme accuracy, or there was an ancient civilization that once inhabited the Earth, greater than ours, that was able to understand things we are just beginning to understand.

Cintra Township Glyphs

Outlined below is the final destination of each radial in the Cintra glyph.

300 Degree Radial - The future site of Jamestown Virginia, USA , first acknowledged
settlement in North America and the location of the Eastern vertex of the Great Triangle.
336 Degree Radial -Baffin Island Harbor
257 Degree Radial -Westernmost point in South America.
293 Degree Radial -Bermuda
259 Degree Radial -Where the Equator crosses the West coast of South America.
340 Degree Radial -Southern Tip of Greenland.
291 Degree Radial -Southern Tip of Texas, USA

351 Degree Radial -Isla De Gomera, Canary Islands. Where explorers begin their voyage westward if using
the Southern route. This included Columbus and de Soto. This island was identified in a 7000 year old Egyptian glyph.
205 Degree Radial -Southern Tip of South America.
208 Degree Radial -Sacred Site South of the Southern tip of South America.

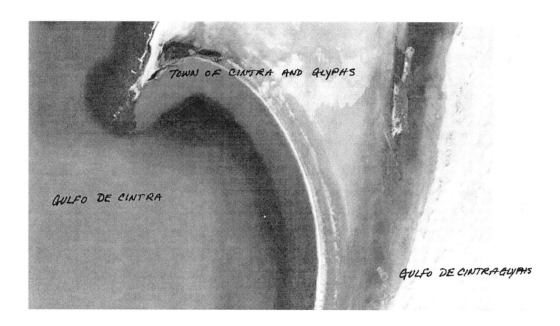

Relative Location of Gulfo de Cintra Glyphs and Cintra Township Glyphs

About five miles to the Northwest of the Gulfo de Cintra Glyphs is located the township of Cintra, Western Sahara, Africa. It is nothing more than a thinly populated fishing village. However it contains glyphs that, although not exactly orientated the same as the Gulfo de Cintra Glyphs, is enough like them to suggest that they are somehow related. You are most likely asking; how did these glyphs survive for as long as they have? I can't speak for the Cintra Township Glyphs because it is not yet known how old they are. However, the Gulfo de Cintra Glyphs are dated by the Nabta Playa Circle as being over 7000 years old. they have survived for the same reason that the Nazca Lines have survived. There is very little rain in this area to erode the glyphs.

The following two photos show circle glyphs located just East of Nabta Playa. These glyphs appear to confirm the validity of the Stone Circle glyph found in Nabta Playa.

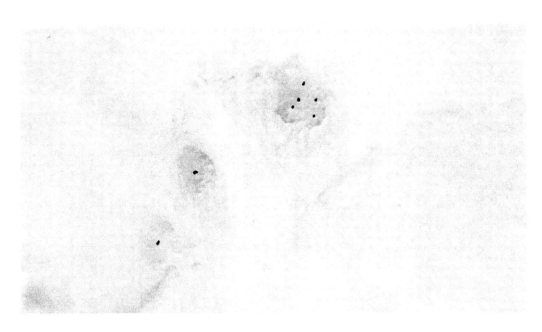

Center points of the Nabta Playa geoglyphs.

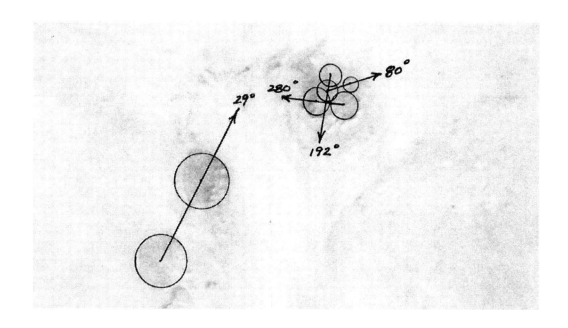

Bearings generated by the Nabta Playa geoglyphs.

Outlined below are the end points of each radial in the Nabta Playa glyph.

029 Degree Radial - Luxor, Karnak, and Valley of the Kings, Egypt
080 Degree Radial -Abu Dahbi, UAI Glyphs
192 Degree Radial -Southern Tip of Africa
280 Degree Radial -Gulfo de Cintra Glyphs

EGYPT 1200AD

BBC Article , The Fall of the Egyptian Old Kingdom - Prof. Fakri Hassan

The Grip of Famine

At a time, in pre-history, the Sahara desert was once a bountiful plain full of animals to hunt and grass for them to graze upon. A shift in weather patterns caused the Sahara to dry up almost overnight. This change forced the surviving people to migrate to the Nile valley as the only water available in North Africa. Their existence became dependent on the Nile flooding each year, and bringing rich soil and nutrients downstream from Ethiopia. Starting c2200 BC poor floods periodically caused distress, famine, plague and civil unrest in Egypt. This was the beginning of the end for the Egyptian Dynasties. Archaeological evidence from the time verifies the famine was so bad people In Northern Egypt were reduced to cannibalism. Again, in AD 967, a lack of flooding caused a severe famine that left 600,000 people dead in and around Fustat, the capital of Egypt at the time. The famine lasted for two years and it was not until AD 971-2 that plentiful harvests returned. Once again, in 1201, low Nile floods followed by another low flood in 1202 caused a catastrophic famine. Interestingly, the Egyptians from the Southern Nile Valley were not affected.

This eyewitness account comes from Abdel-Latif Al-Baghdadi, a physician/scholar from Baghdad who was in Egypt from 1194 to AD 1200. He reported that people left Egypt by the thousands and that those who remained habitually ate human flesh; parents even ate their own children. Graves were ransacked for food, assassinations and robbery reigned unchecked and noblewomen implored to be bought as slaves. Al-Baghdadi's account is almost an exact copy of that recorded by Ankhtifi, more than 3000 years earlier.

All Upper Egypt was dying of hunger, to such an extent that everyone has come to eating his children ... The entire country had become starved like a starved grasshopper, with people going to the north and to the south (in search of grain). There is evidence that some previous droughts were even more severe than these. (Al-Baghdadi, a physician / scholar from Baghdad)

The low Nile episode that devastated the Old Kingdom was, however, of greater magnitude and duration than that of 967 or AD 1201. (Al-Baghdadi, a physician / scholar from Baghdad)

History tells us that the Mayan civilization in Yucatan Mexico came into being in the first millennium BC. The Mayans can be tied to the Egyptians through the identical use geoglyphs in the construction of their pyramids. This commonality could not be a coincidence as some would have you believe up until now. Through the Stonehenge Monument we have established that the Celts knew of the existence of the Americas at least as early as 3100 BC. It is therefore no stretch to consider that the Celts rescued starving Egyptians, from which they were most likely descended, and transplanted them to Central America to save them from death, or to colonize the New World which they may have considered their own.

THE SECRET OF THE PYRAMIDS

As indicated before, the extended north line of Nabta Playa extends through what would later be the site of the pyramids of Khui, Amenemhet III, and the city of Cairo. Having measured the angles on just about every major monument on Earth it was inevitable that we would eventually come to the Pyramids in Egypt. As you will learn in later chapters, the Pyramids in Mexico, and China exhibit the same geometrical properties that exist in the Egyptian pyramids. The architecture in all these structures exhibit the use of the same architectural protocols in their alignments. That is, their alignments outline specific territories, many of which have been carried over into modern times and exist today, with minor deviations.

The Great Pyramids of Egypt

All my life I have heard about how perfectly the Egyptian Pyramids are aligned North and South. The results that we achieved by using satellite photos and computer programs confirms this. This accuracy also applies to all the geoglyphs which we have located around the world. In determining whether the Egyptian Pyramids had any useful geoglyphic alignments, we began plotting the sides of the Pyramid that run North and South and East and West. Those pointed exactly nowhere. Disproving the argument that you can draw any line and it will go somewhere of importance. As you can observe in the photo above there are only two bearings that were derived from this particular pyramid. That is because the two bearings extending from the West side of the Pyramid do not intersect any significant geographical point before they circumnavigate half the Earth and reverse to become the reciprocal bearings from the East side.

That brings up an important point, most glyph sites have a theme. The radials on one Glyph site might point primarily to rivers, others might point to harbors, peninsulas, or significant points on a continent, islands, etc. This is most likely done to verify what type of termination point is associated with that particular glyph. It is easier to locate the termination point of radials emanating from any particular Glyph because they are associated with one another. In this case, since it is the Egyptian Pyramids, the pointers should point to something significant. The two bearings emanating from the East side of the Pyramid point to the tip of two continents. The tip of two continents would be considered pretty significant. (See below) During our previous studies we determined that the tip of Baja California is consistently used to denote a crucial point in the North American territory and was once considered part of what is now the United States. The North American territory will be reviewed in a later chapter. The tip of Baja California and the tip of South America are referenced in scores of glyphs located around the world.

The end point of the 045 degree bearing from the Giza Pyramid.

The end point of the 135 degree bearing from the Giza Pyramid.

Now that we had discovered that the pyramid is pointing to two significant points on the Earth, the tip of Baja California and the Southern tip of South America, we figured we must be on to something, but we were not sure what. (Isn't it interesting that Baja Peninsula is referred to on maps as Baja California and not Mexico?) Surely a culture that had built the largest structure in the world would have more to offer. The only clues we had so far were the end points from the pyramid bearings, the tip of Baja and the tip of South America. But we had also been given the bearings of 135 degrees and 045 degrees. We decided to use these bearings starting from the tip of Baja and the tip of South America to see where they pointed. The results appear in the next Plate.

The end point of the 135 degree bearing from the tip of South America.

As you can see, we were on the right track. The 135 degree bearing landed on the tip of India. Curiously, India has played a major role in history as an innovator and recorder of ancient information. Most people think that the English alphabet originated in Arabia, it actually originated in India. India also originated the concept of the number zero (0), without which we would have no mathematics or computers.

The path of the 045 degree bearing from the Tip of Baja.

We then ran the 045 bearing from Baja. I was disappointed to see it crossed the boundary of Galicia without crossing a significant geographical landmark. From previous study I knew that Galicia, the first country formed in Europe and now part of Spain, was, at the time it was founded, a Celtic stronghold. Our studies show that the Celts were, most likely, descended from the Egyptians, I hoped that, after further study, this line terminating in Galicia would come to mean something. It was then that we ran a 45 degree radial from the Southern tip of South America.

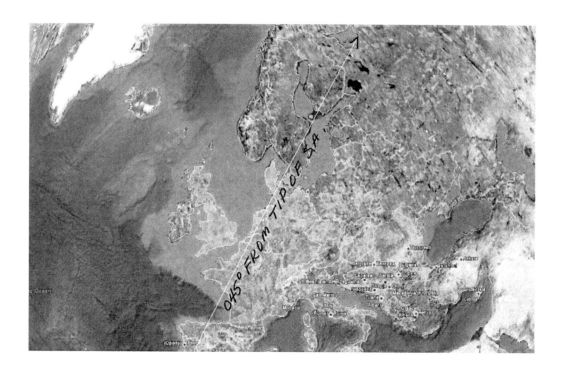

The path of the 045 degree bearing from the Tip of South America.

Well, things were looking up. After plotting the path of the 045 degree bearing from the Tip of South America it crossed the Galician Coast at precisely the same point as the 045 degree bearing from the tip of Baja. You may be asking; how can two radials of the same bearing cross at the same point? The answer is that any two, non-parallel lines will always cross somewhere on a round surface. However, an intelligent, or extremely lucky random placement, can cause these two lines to cross at a predetermined point. This, in itself, led us to believe there was something to be learned from this oddity.

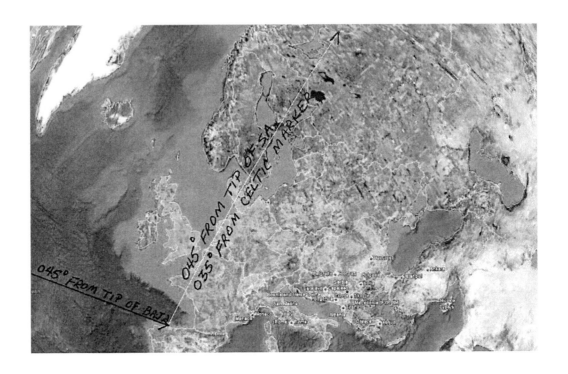

This plate illustrates the boundaries formed by the two 045 degree bearings.

Although both 045 degree bearings pointed to a place in a Celtic country, we were at a loss as to why this was significant. We needed verification that this was a correct solution to these two 45 degree radials. As stated several times before, the originators of these geoglyphs always backup their work with checks and balances. That is when we decided to look on the ground. Sure enough, as you see in the photo below, there was a glyph on the ground which verified that this was a proper solution to the riddle. On the ground, next to the ink lines, you can see the two raised linier mounds that coincide with, and validate, the two 045 degree bearings that they represent.

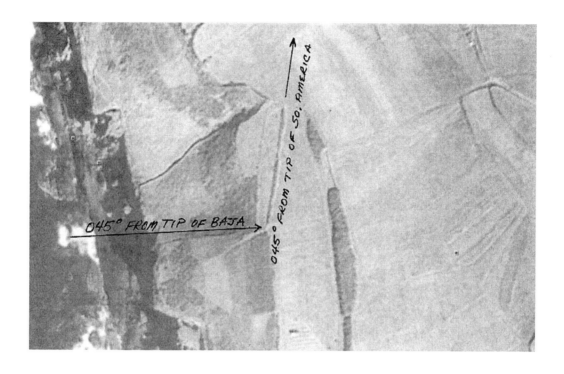

This Plate shows the geoglyph on the ground that corresponds to the
045 degree bearings that it mirrors.

This Map Shows the Countries and Territory Occupied by a Coordinated Celtic Empire c1400.

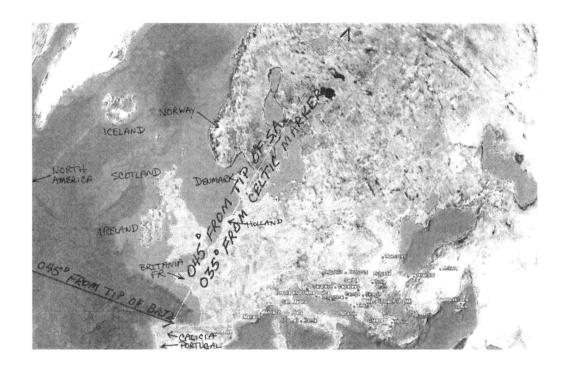

The Pre-Columbian Galician/Celtic Empire.

The two Plates above show the boundaries of a territory designated by the geometry of the Giza Pyramid. This area eventually evolved into what became a Galician, then a Celtic, a Catholic, and eventually a Protestant Empire. The inhabitants living west of these lines considered the boundaries formed by the two 045 degree radials very important. Once the Celts were pushed over the 45 degree boundaries, by other Europeans, they fought to maintain this empire from all who tried to conquer it. That included, in particular, the Catholic Church. The next Plate depicts the radials generated by the Stonehenge monolith in the UK. If you will notice the only point identified, in what is now the United States, is the North American survey marker Inspiration Peak. That is because Inspiration Peak is where the North American survey marker originates. As you will notice later the two territories do not overlap. (This will be covered in more detail in the Chapter titled "The Vikings in America".

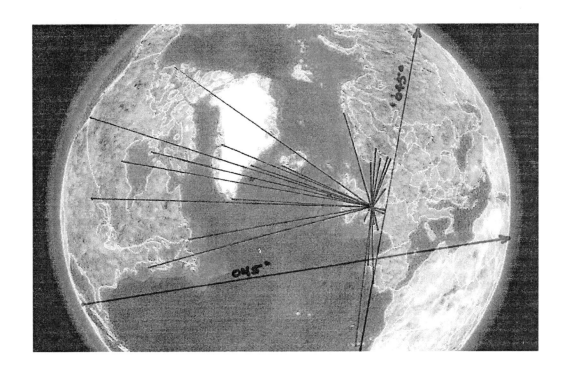

The Stonehenge Radials, and Endpoints, Relative to the Giza 45 Degree Radials

The above photo validates the premise that the 45 Degree radials, generated from information originating at the Giza Pyramid, were to designate a territory that would eventually be settled by members of the Celtic Clans. Wars and evolution would eventually mold this area into an area of modern cooperation with a defense alliance to protect the inhabitants on the West side of the 45 Degree Radial from the peoples who lived on the East side.

The format of the geometric information at Giza is identical to the methods used in monoliths built, down through history, by the early Japanese, Turks, Chinese, Celts, Mayans, South Americans, Portuguese, Mississippians, Nordics, and early colonists of the Americas. This cannot be a coincidence, especially since this method has remained a secret until now. This indicates that a segment of all the ancient cultures had an ancient knowledge, available to only a few trusted individuals, that has been passed down from long before recorded history. Since this protocol shows up primarily in structures, it would be safe to assume the persons passing this information along would be the builders of the structures, the Masons. Now that you know this, it answers many questions about why the capitol of the United States, and its money, is fraught with Egyptian symbols, monoliths and geoglyphs which, until now, organizations such as the Masons have been protecting.

Notice should be taken that the location of the Giza pyramid is one of the few places on the face of the earth where all the radials derived from a square would point to their intended targets. This means that all the continents of the world were known to the builders of the pyramids in 2560 BC when the pyramids were built, and based on the 7000 year old Gulfo de Cintra Glyphs, long before that. The incredible accuracy of orientations displayed in monoliths around the globe mirrors the incredible accuracy in the alignment of the base of the Pyramids. Recent study indicates that various geometrical extensions of the Giza radials could also outline other territories. This is still being studied.

The Secret of Luxor

Luxor was the ancient city of Thebes, the great capital of Egypt during the New Kingdom, and the glorious city of the god Amen. As the city of the god Amen, Thebes remained the religious capital of Egypt until the Greek period. The god of the city was Amen, who was worshipped together with his wife, the Goddess Mut, and their son Khonsu. With the rise of Thebes as the foremost city of Egypt, the local god Amen (Also known as Amun and Amon) rose in importance as well and became linked to the sun god Ra, thus creating the new 'king of gods' Amon-Ra. His great temple, at Karnak just north of Thebes, was the most important temple of Egypt right until the end of antiquity. Immediately opposite, across the River Nile, lie the monuments, temples and tombs on the West Bank Necropolis, which include the Valley of the Kings and Valley of the Queens.

What you are about to experience is unexplainable but leaves only a few incredible avenues of explanation open to discussion. While exploring the many South American geoglyphs we noticed two gigantic meteor craters, one at the North end of South America and one at the South end of South America. What was so interesting was that both craters seemed to be almost identical. I'm sure the existence of these craters have been known for as long as man has been able to map the ocean floor, but these were too identical to ignore. It is a known fact that if the Gulf Stream were to quit running, from the Pacific to Greenland, the loss of warm water that it carries to the North Atlantic would cause another Ice Age. That caused us to wonder what the Earth was like before these two impacts opened up the flow of currents from the Pacific to the Atlantic. There most likely would have been a severe Ice Age. We then begin to ask ourselves how two meteor impacts that obviously came from approximately the same direction, of approximately the same mass, rotating to the right, like a bullet for stability, could land at exactly the only two places in the world that could open up the flow of current from the Pacific Ocean to the Atlantic Ocean. This would have initiated what we now call the Gulf Stream, thereby causing the ice to recede and introducing a more moderate climate for the existence of mankind on the Earth. It looked too much like divine intervention.

It looked like a Duck, so we decided to see if it quacked like one. If you have trouble seeing the entire Northern impact crater take a look at the next photo and notice the difference in the color of the earth running through Colombia and Venezuela. It is presumed the reason that the Northern passageway is no longer open is because of the geological rift running around the Pacific Rim. This rift would cause the land mass that was carved out by the Northern impact to rise again and block this passageway from the Pacific to the Atlantic. Even with this geological intervention the area around where the Panama Canal was built was almost passable. At the time the canal was constructed the area consisted of lakes and swamps. It did not take long before we discovered some interesting facts, about the alignments and geometry of the craters. What we found would astound us.

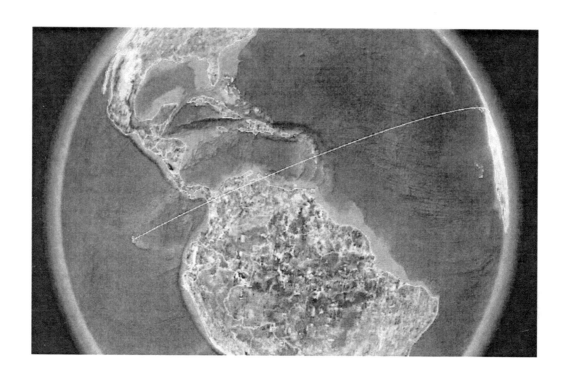

**A 60 degree bearing running from the Galapagos Islands
through the center of the Northern impact crater**

The end point of the 60 degree bearing from the Galapagos Islands.

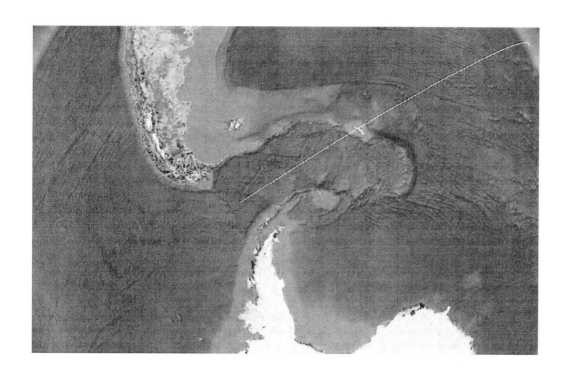

A 60 degree bearing, as measured at the Trident (Explained below), and starting at the center of the Southern impact crater

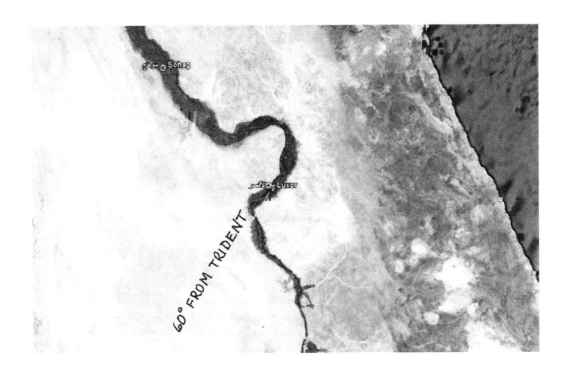

The end point of a 60 degree bearing, running from the center of the Southern impact crater, through the Trident and ending at Luxor. (The Trident is explained below)

Spherical Geometry

It is difficult to grasp the concept that two parallel headings can cross. This is largely due to the way we are used to thinking in terms of Plane Geometry on a flat plane. However, this changes when you draw lines on a sphere. In dealing with a sphere you enter the realm of Spherical Geometry. In Spherical Geometry there are no parallel lines.

Spherical Geometry is the study of figures on the surface of a sphere, as opposed to the type of geometry studied in plane geometry or solid geometry. In spherical geometry, straight lines are great circles, so any two lines will meet in two places. There are also no parallel lines. The angle between two lines in spherical geometry is the angle between the planes of the corresponding great circles, and a spherical triangle is defined by its three angles. There is no concept of similar triangles in plane geometry.

In the field of Geoglyphology, we are working in a spherical world and plotting on a flat plane. Therefore, it is difficult to grasp the concept of combining Spherical Geometry with Plane Geometry. This is why the field of Geoglyphology could not have been proposed without the advent of software that computes using Spherical Geometry while displaying it on a flat plane. All calculations for this book were arrived at by using "Google Earth Pro".

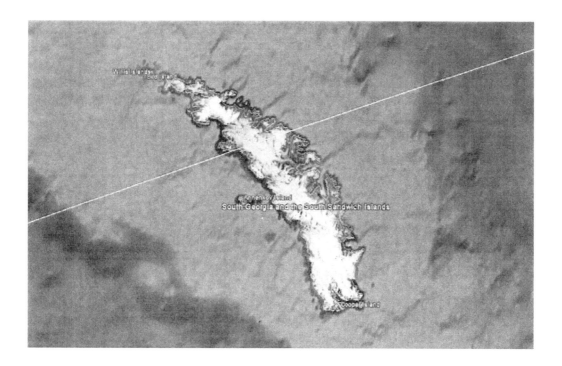

Saint George Island, also seen in the third photo above.

**A mountain on Saint George Island called the Trident. The bearing
from this point to Luxor is also 60 degrees.**

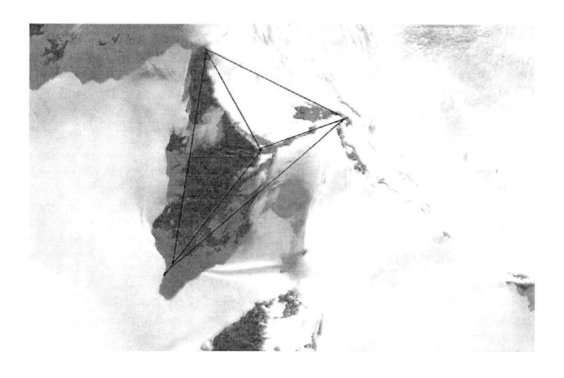

A depiction of how the mountain forms a three sided pyramid, thereby earning the name "The Trident".

As you can see, from the above photos, the alignment of the two meteor craters does not appear to be random. This opens up a host of other questions, not the least of which is; Who, or what, has the skill and power to initiate and execute such a massive undertaking? Scientists have said for years that the Northern meteor impact was what killed the dinosaurs. Did the Southern meteor impact cause the great flood? If the alignments of the impacts were random, where did the ancients get the skill to know where the two 060 degree radials crossed, or that there were impact craters on the ocean floor that they could use to locate Luxor, their spiritual capitol?

Incredible similarities between the two impact craters:

1. The meteor craters appear almost identical. This would seem to indicate objects of similar size, both rotating to the right for stability, like a bullet.
2. Both impacts open up the flow of current from the Pacific to the Atlantic. (Now named the Gulf Stream. Could this be because it used to flow into the Gulf from the Pacific?)
3. Radials running through the center of both impact craters have bearings of 060 degrees.
4. Both 060 degree bearings originate from islands formed by the meteor impacts.
5. The 060 degree bearings from both craters point to Luxor, Egypt, the spiritual center of ancient Egypt.
6. The Southern 060 degree radial initiates at a pyramid. The Pyramid became an important symbol to the Egyptians and their descendents.
7. The Trident seems to form two Right Triangles and one Equilateral Triangle. Both the Right Triangle and the Equilateral Triangle play an important part in the geometry of geoglyphs down through time.

This makes you wonder who had the power and technology to initiate something of this magnitude, and who had the technical knowledge to work out the geometry after the impacts.

END CHAPTER

Chapter 4

The Chinese Pyramids

Pyramid Tomb of Emperor Jing, with sharp edges of pyramid eroded away

The pyramid covering the tomb of Emperor Jing of Han (r. 156-141 BCE), located outside of Xi'an China, is just one of the many dirt pyramids in the area. Chinese pyramids are ancient mausoleums built to house the remains of several early emperors of China and their imperial relatives. About 38 of them are located around 25 kilometers (16 mi) - 35 kilometers (22 mi) north-west of Xi'an, on the Qin Chuan Plains in Shaanxi Province. The most famous is the Mausoleum of the First Qin Emperor, northeast of Xi'an and 1.7 km west of where the Terracotta Warriors were found. Chinese pyramids were also built during the Xia Dynasty 2194 BC - 1600 BC, the Han Dynasty 206BC -220 AD, the Tang Dynasty 618 ad - 907 AD, and the Sung Dynasty 960 - 1279 AD.

They have flat tops, and thus are more similar in shape to the Teotihuacan pyramids north-east of Mexico City, Mexico than to the pyramids in Giza, Egypt. Although known in the West for at least a century, their existence has been made controversial by sensationalist publicity and the problems of Chinese archaeology in early 20th century.

Pottery figurines of domesticated animals and female servants dressed in silk robes were excavated from the mausoleum of Emperor Jing of Han (Circa 156-141 BC) near modern Xi'an (ancient Chang'an). The introduction of pyramids in China to the world came in two stages. Many early stories were focused on the existence of "Great White Pyramid." U.S. Army Air Corps pilot James Gaussman is said to have seen a white jewel-topped pyramid during a flight between India and China during World War II. Colonel Maurice Sheahan, Far Eastern director of Trans World Airlines, told an eyewitness account of his encounter with a pyramid in the March 28, 1947 edition of The New York Times. A photo of Sheahan's pyramid appeared in The New York Sunday News on March 30, 1947. This photograph later became attributed to James Gaussman. Chris Maier showed that the pyramid in the photo is the Maoling Mausoleum of Emperor Wu of Han, just outside of Xi'an. Alternative writers such as Hartwig Hausdorf and Phillip Coppens did much to bring them to public attention.

Despite claims to the contrary, the existence of these pyramid-shaped tomb mounds was known by scientists in the West before the publicity caused by the story in 1947. Shortly after the New York Times story, Science News Letter (now Science News) published a short item saying "The Chinese pyramids of that region are built of mud and dirt and are more like mounds than the pyramids of Egypt, and the region is little traveled. American scientists, who have been in the area, suggest that the height of 1,000 feet (300 m), more than twice as high as any of the Egyptian pyramids, may have been exaggerated, because most of the Chinese mounds of that area are built relatively low. The location, reported 40 miles (64 km) southwest of Sian, is in an area of great archaeological importance, but few of the pyramids have ever been explored. Victor Segalen visited China in 1913 and wrote about the First Emperor's tomb (and other mound tombs in the region) in Mission Archeologique en Chine (1914): L'art funeraire a l'epoque des Han. Some of the pyramids of Xi'an are now tourist attractions and several pyramids have small museums attached to them.

THE MOUND TOMBS IN CHINA

Xi'an, Location of the Chinese Pyramids

Partial list of Chinese pyramids in the Xi'an area where the majority of Chinese pyramids reside.

Pyramid 1: 34°20'17N 108°34'11E
Pyramid 6: 34°21'47N 108°37'50E
Pyramid 7: 34°21'42N 108°38'24E
Pyramid 11: 34°22'30N 108°41'53E
Pyramid 15: 34°23'52N 108°42'45E
Pyramid 31: 34°14'09N 109°07'07E
Pyramids 33,34,35: 34°10'52N 109°01'20E
Another: 34°22'47N 108°42'16E
Another: 34°24'03N 108°45'53E
Another: 34°13'16N 109°05'47E
Huang-ti Mausoleum 37: 34°22'52N 109°15'14E

Mount Li mausoleum is the largest Chinese pyramid. The original height is 76 meters (249 ft), the present height is 47 meters (154 ft), and the size is 357 meters (1,171 ft) x 354 meters (1,161 ft). It was built during the short-lived imperial Qin Dynasty (221-206 BC).

Maoling mausoleum (or Great White Pyramid) is the second largest Chinese pyramid. The size is 222 meters (728 ft) x 217 meters (712 ft). It contains the tombs of emperor Wudi (156-87 BC) of the Han Dynasty (206 BC - 220 AD) and some family members and protégés.

There are eighteen mausoleums of the Tang Dynasty emperors, in the valley of the Wei River north of the Qinling Mountains. Some are among the biggest Chinese mausoleums, such as Qianling, joint tomb of Emperor Gaozong of Tang and of the Empress Wu Zetian. It is a natural hill shaped by man.

Janggun-chong is a step Pyramid in Jilin, "Tomb of the General", is supposed to be the mausoleum of King Jangsu (413-491 AD), king of Goguryeo, an ancient Korean kingdom. It belongs to the Capital Cities and Tombs of the Ancient Koguryo Kingdom on the World heritage list. Nearby is the Taewang-neung Pyramid believed to be the burial of King Gwanggaeto the Great (391-413 AD); while twice bigger than Janggun-chong, it is in bad shape and Janggun-chong is touted as the touristic highpoint of the site.

The Western Xia tombs of the Tangut Empire near Yinchuan in Ningxia Hui Autonomous Region, northwestern China, a large number of tombs covering some 50 km2 (19 sq mi) are referred to as 'Chinese Pyramids'.

Even though these pyramids were built in China they have undeniable ties to the geoglyphs in Europe, North America and Mexico. Different cultures tend to construct pyramids from the materials at hand. In the case of China it was earthen. None the less, the architectural similarities to the Mexican Pyramids cannot be denied. In addition, the builders of these pyramids maintained their ties to their North American locations, and geoglyphs, by incorporating the same geometric principles which point to locations previously identified and marked in North America. This is just one more signpost that proves that the construction of many pyramids around the world are related. The proof of this is exhibited in the orientations and pointers that are included in the architecture of the Chinese pyramids which appear in the photos below:

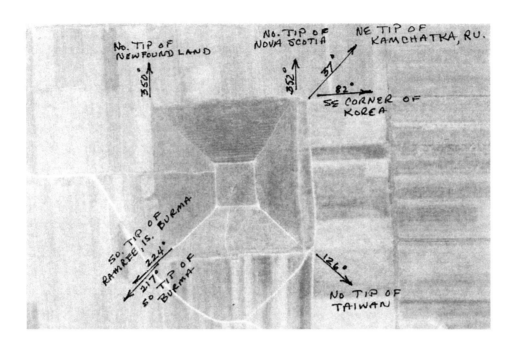

Chinese Pyramid #6

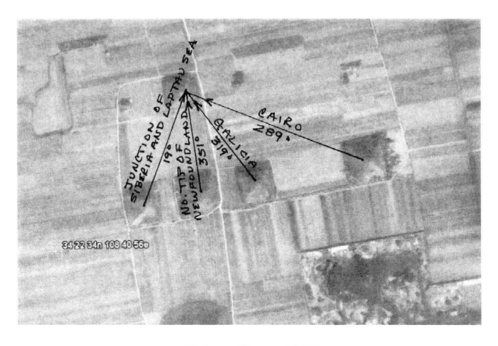

Chinese Pyramid #8

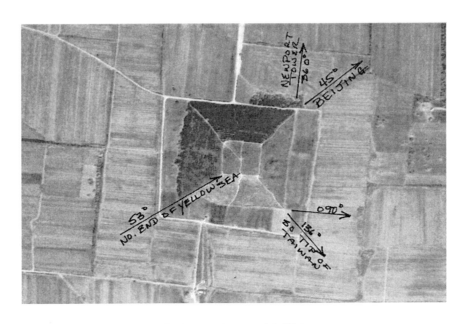

Chinese Pyramid #21

Chinese Pyramid #31

END CHAPTER

Chapter 5

The Pyramids of Mexico

THE MAYAN CIVALIZATION

The Mayan Civilization was a Mesoamerican culture, noted for the only known fully developed written language of the pre-Columbian Americas, as well as its art, architecture, and mathematical and astronomical systems. Initially established during the Pre-Classic period (c. 2000 BC to 250 AD), according to the Mesoamerican chronology, many Maya cities reached their highest state of development during the Classic period (c. 250 AD to 900 AD), and continued throughout the Post-Classic period until the arrival of the Spanish. At its peak, it was one of the most densely populated and culturally dynamic societies in the world.

The Mayan civilization shares many features with other Mesoamerican civilizations due to the high degree of interaction and cultural diffusion that characterized the region. Although writing, epigraphy, and the calendar did not originate with the Maya, their civilization fully developed them. Maya influence can be detected from Honduras, Guatemala, El Salvador and to as far as central Mexico, more than 1000 km (625 miles) from the Maya area. Many outside influences are found in Mayan art and architecture, which are thought to result from trade and cultural exchange rather than direct conquest.

The geographic extent of the Mayan civilization, known as the Maya area, extended throughout the southern Mexican states of Chiapas, Tabasco, and the Yucatán Peninsula states of Quintana Roo, Campeche and Yucatán. The Maya area also extended throughout the northern Central American region, including the present-day nations of Guatemala, Belize, El Salvador and western Honduras.

Construction

The Classic period (c. 250–900 AD) witnessed the peak of large-scale construction and urbanism, the recording of monumental inscriptions, and a period of significant intellectual and artistic development, particularly in the southern lowland regions. The most notable monuments are the stepped pyramids where they built their religious centers and the accompanying palaces of their rulers. The palace at Cancuen is the largest in the Maya area, though the site, interestingly, lacks pyramids. Other important archaeological remains include the carved stone slabs usually called stelae (the Maya called them tetun, or "tree-stones"), which depict rulers along with hieroglyphic texts describing their genealogy, military victories, and other accomplishments.

Pyramids and Temples

Though city layouts evolved as nature dictated, careful attention was placed on the directional orientation of temples and observatories. Often the most important religious temples sat atop the towering Maya pyramids, presumably as the closest place to the heavens. While recent discoveries point toward the extensive use of pyramids as tombs, the temples themselves seem to rarely, if ever, contain burials. Residing atop the pyramids, some are over two-hundred feet tall, are temples such as that at El Mirador. The temples were impressive and decorated structures themselves. Commonly topped with a roof comb, these temples might have served as a type of propaganda as they were often the only structure in a Maya city to exceed the height of the surrounding jungle. The roof combs atop the temples were often carved with representations of rulers that could be seen from vast distances.

Observatories

The Maya were keen astronomers and had mapped out the phases of celestial objects, especially the Moon and Venus. Many temples have doorways and other features aligning to celestial events. Round temples, often dedicated to Kukulcan, are perhaps those most often described as "observatories" by modern ruin tour-guides, but there is no evidence that they were so used exclusively, and temple pyramids of other shapes may well have been used for observation as well.

A COMMON LINK

The Pyramids

There has been much speculation as to who was responsible for building of the pyramids in Mexico. Research has shown that the Mayans were a multi-cultural society. This would lend itself to a cooperative project to build the pyramids. However, the technology and desire to the build pyramids could not have happened overnight. There should have been a period of progression and experimentation leading up to the building of the final monoliths. This progression exists in Egypt but is not found in Mesoamerica. Logic would dictate that there was most likely an external influence that caused similar pyramids, and monoliths, to have been built around the world during a period in time that coincides with the decline of the Egyptian Empire and the great famines of the Nile Valley. It would be easy for the architects of the pyramids to incorporate subtle, self serving, messages into the pyramid orientation which may have gone unnoticed by the actual builders. Regardless of who the people were that built the Mayan pyramids, it will become quite obvious from the data shown below that there was some degree of Egyptian influence in the process. By applying the same measuring principles applied to Stonehenge, Inspiration Peak, the Egyptian Pyramids, and glyph sites around the globe, there can be no doubt that the same mindset existed in the building of all of the these structures.

The pointers that are found in the Mexican pyramids, built around 100 BC, point to the same places as glyph sites made thousands of years earlier by their predecessors and hundreds of years later by their descendants. From recently discovered monoliths around the world we can draw no other conclusion than that a common thread has existed that ties architecture, geoglyphs, and the marking of territorial boundaries around the world together for at least ten millennia. One would have to ask how did they do it and where did they obtain their knowledge. I will leave the answer to that question to others, but it does present some interesting possibilities.

For those that are still having trouble with the idea that the Mayan pyramids were built by Egyptians here is an excerpt from Gavin Menzie's well researched book "1421, The Year The Chinese Discovered America":

Menzies writes: *"When the Chinese met the people of Mexico it is highly probable that they would have been shown Palenque, the finest Mayan city. At the time, Phaenque would have appeared to the Chinese as the work of a people whose talent equaled their own. ... Here is everything the archaeologist or historian could wish for: the fabulous tomb of a 'Pharaoh of the jungle', filled with treasures; palaces of Kings and priests covered in hieroglyphics telling the story of the site; observatories, temples, and ball courts... . The extraordinary white pyramid of King Pakal dominates the site. The Cuban scholar Alberto Ruz Lhuillier spent years digging down a secret stairway into the chamber at the very bottom. In 1952 his team wrenched aside a huge stone and entered a darkened vault."*

Lhuillier writes: *"Out of the dim shadows emerged a vision from a fairytale, a fantastic ethereal sight from another world. It seemed a huge magic grotto, carved out of ice, the walls sparkling and glistening like snow crystals... the impression in fact, was that of an abandoned chapel. Across the walls marched stucco figures in low relief. Then my eyes sought the floor. This was almost entirely filled with the great carved stone slab, in perfect condition... Ours were the first eyes that gazed upon it for more than a thousand years."*

It was then that they spotted the burial vault. In feverish excitement, Lhuillier and his team opened the lid and peered inside.

Lhuillier writes: "My first impression was that of a mosaic of green, red and white. Then it resolved itself into details - green jade ornaments, red painted teeth and bones, and a fragment of the mask. I was gazing at the death [mask] of him for whom all this stupendous work - the crypt, the sculpture, the stairway, the great pyramid with its crowning temple - had been built... This then was a sarcophagus, the first ever found in a Mayan pyramid."

Menzies writes: *"The beautifully proportioned pyramid with its simple, smoothly faced stone, the hidden stairway, the interior crypt and the superb mask and jewelry are the work of a people of immense architectural, engineering and artistic talent."*

Anyone that has had experience with Egyptian burial sites will see that this description sounds very much like a burial chamber in the Valley of the kings.

Pyramid locations in the Yucatan

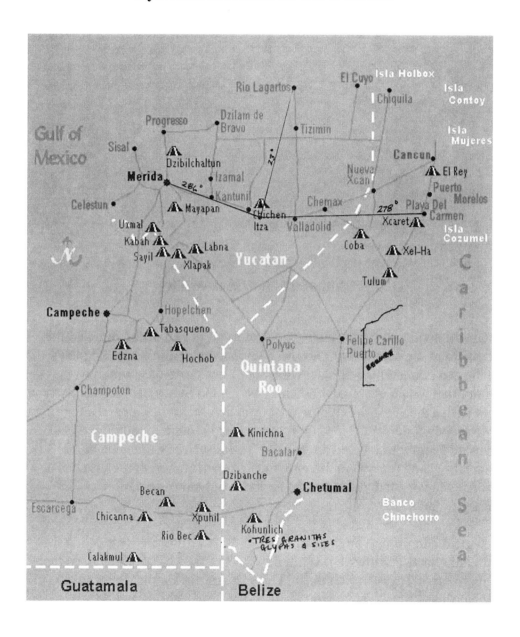

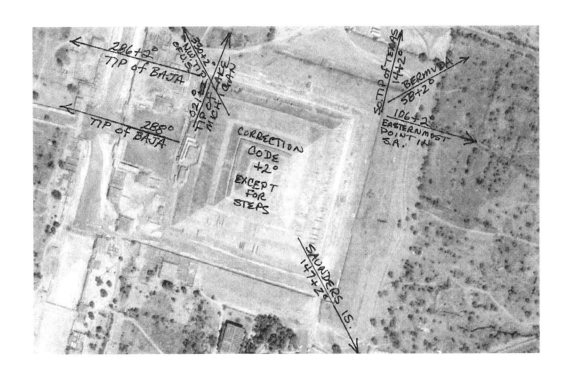

Pyramid of the Sun, Mexico City

If you will notice, in the previous photo of the Pyramid of the Sun and the next photo of the complex at Oaxaca, Mexico, the pyramids are aligned so that the end points of the radials, which their design creates, outline a territory that would eventually become the United States of America. As you might notice this geoglyph requires a correction factor of 2 degrees to bring it into proper alignment. This correction factor is found in only the most important geoglyphs located around the world, such as Stonehenge. It is presumably done to prevent the unworthy from deciphering the glyph. The correction factor can be determined by the geoglyphs orientation to True North.

From the diagrams one might ask; "Why is Baja California included in the North American Territory but is not now part of the US, and how does the Southern tip of Texas fit into this?" The answers are simple. From glyphs all over North and South America it is clear that Baja California, and Mesoamerica, were originally intended to be part of the North American Territory. This plan was foiled by the invasion of Mexico by Hernando Cortes in 1515. As you may remember from your US history, Spain then colonized Central America and the Western US. The Western US was won back in the War with Mexico, however, Baja California remained Mexican territory. This story is covered in the final chapter of this book.

As inconsequential as the Southern tip of Texas may seem, in ancient and colonial times, it was a very important point of reference. Surprisingly the Southern tip of Texas, with it's numerous undocumented geoglyphs, was the most referenced spot on the globe when considering geoglyphs which were constructed in the last 2000 years. The Southern Texas geoglyphs are also referenced in the last chapter of this book.

Monte Alban Pyramid #1, Oaxaca, Mexico

Castillo, Chichin Itza, Yucatan, Mexico

ANCIENT MEXICO CITY

When I first viewed a map of the ancient city of Mexico City I was amazed. After deciphering hundreds of Egyptian and Celtic glyphs the pattern formed by the causeways of Mexico City jumped out at me. Could I dare believe that this ancient city was a glyph itself. If it was, it would prove beyond any doubt that there was a connection between the Egyptians and early European inhabitants of North and Central America. As I begin my evaluation my hands were trembling with excitement. As it turned out the city was a giant geoglyph that outlined the very landmass that I had suspected all along to be the original plan for the formation of a territory in North America.

In the first diagram below is the city oriented as it actually was. The radials that emanate from the causeway orientations point to various landmarks that outline the Southern boundary of a territory in North America. (Explained below.) But that was not the amazing part. When I viewed the original orientation I noticed two things that were out of place. First of all the writing on the map was upside down when you place North at the top. Secondly, with North at the top, the East/West orientation line pointed West. It is well known that maps of this period were oriented East. So now I am confronted by a map made in 1524 with writing upside down and the primary orientation line on the left side instead of the right.

After deciphering the map in its original orientation (Results below) I remembered the Nabta Playa Glyph in Southern Egypt. That glyph required that the glyph be flipped over before it gave up it's secret. Could that be the case here? Rather than flipping the map over I first tried just rotating it until the West pointer was pointing East. Sure enough a deciphering of the resulting radials showed that they pointed to places that I had seen hundreds of times before in other Celtic and Egyptian geoglyphs. Of these radials, only two pointed to spots that would later become important in US history. However, the remaining radials did point to locations seen many times before in other geoglyphs located around the world.

By this time I was in a daze. I realized the technical skills that would be required to set up a geometrical puzzle of this magnitude. What minds could have figured out one glyph that would conform to two sets of criteria. The two solutions to the Mexico City glyphs are depicted in the following Plates.

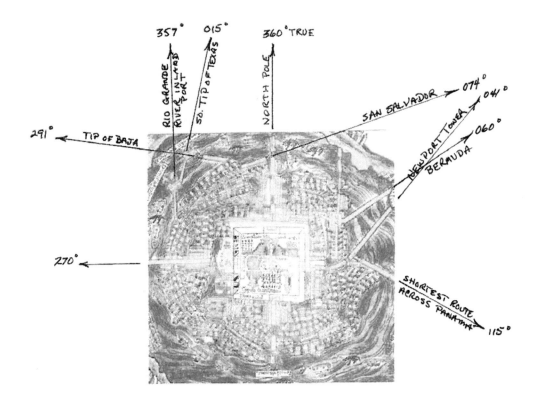

Ancient Mexico City as it was in 1524, 5 years after the invasion by Cortes.

This is the actual alignment of the causeways of Mexico City at the time Cortes entered Mexico City. As you can see, the primary purpose of this geoglyph is to outline the Southern boundary of the North American Territory and to point the reader to the Newport Tower where, if it's secret were deciphered, the remaining boundaries of the Northern Territories could be found. This is why the Kensington Runestone was carved. Without the information inscribed on the Kensington Runestone the boundaries of the Northern Territory could not be known, even if the location of Inspiration Peak were located using the Newport Tower. (If this seems confusing it is all explained in the Chapter titled "The Newport Tower and The Kensington Runestone".

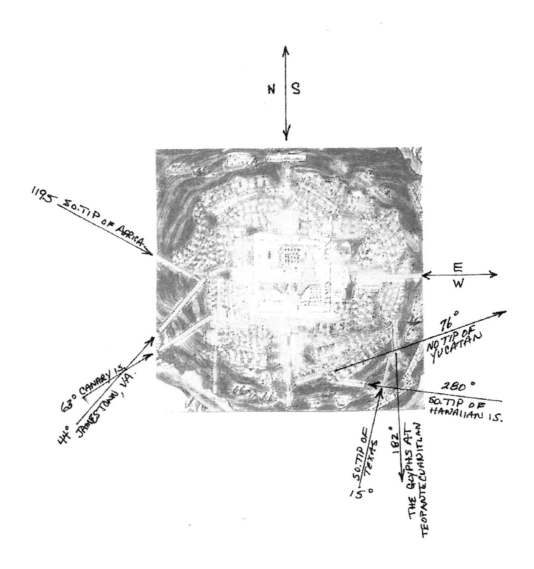

The Mexico City geoglyph rotated 180 degrees.

This orientation of the Mexico City geoglyph provides two locations that would later be important in the history of North America, Jamestown and the Southern tip of Texas. The remaining pointers locate other known geoglyphs that have been important to geoglyph makers for thousands of years. It also points out the Canary Islands which was in antiquity, and is to this day, the supply port and jumping off spot for ships sailing from Europe to the Caribbean.

THE CANARY ISLANDS by Namaste Peter - 2010.

In most maps and geoglyphs that deal with the Caribbean, or North and South America, the Canary Islands are depicted. The reason for this is that the Canary Islands have been used as the supply port for most ships sailing from Europe and Africa to the West for over 7000 years. Some of the history of the Canaries is presented in the following story:

"The Canary Islands became home to a mysterious group of Nordics who became known as the Guanches. While it is unknown for sure how they arrived on the islands, what is known is that they shared a number of cultural characteristics with the ancient Egyptians and that their building style appears to have been replicated in South and Central America.

Like the Celtic Tocharians, the finest evidence of what these original Guanche Nordics looked like, is in the fortuitous existence of original Guanche mummies, which are on public display in the Canary Island national museum. The corpses on display are estimated to be between 600 and 1000 years old. An examination of one of the mummies' bodies showed incisions that virtually matched those found in Egyptian mummies, although the string used by the Guanche embalmers to close the wounds was much coarser than would have been used by the Egyptian experts. The Guanches also possessed the art of writing, although this has not yet been the subject of any major study. The Guanche mummies have red hair and Nordic features.

The most stunning link between the Guanches and the Egyptians comes in the form of pyramids. The Guanches built several small step pyramids on the islands, using exactly the same model as those found in ancient Egypt and in Mesopotamia. The pyramids have an east-west alignment which also indicates that they probably had a religious purpose, associated with the rise and setting of the sun. Thor Heyerdahl, who "rediscovered" the pyramids on the Canary Islands and who set up an academic body to study the phenomena, argued that the pyramids may be remains from explorers who sailed the Atlantic in ancient times, and who may have possibly forged a link with the pre-Columbian civilizations of the Americas. As the original inhabitants of the Canary Islands were fair-haired and bearded, it was possible, Heyerdahl suggested, that long before the 15th Century, people of the same stock as those who settled the Canary Islands, also sailed the same route along the Canary Current that took Christopher Columbus to the Americas.

This theory formed the basis of Heyerdahl's famous "RA" expeditions in which he showed that is was possible to cross the Atlantic in an Egyptian reed boat. In fact Columbus' starting off point was the Canary Islands, where he obtained supplies and water on the island of Gomera, the island next to Tenerife. Gomera is the same island pointed out in the Gulfo de Cintra geoglyph 7000 years earlier. The Guanches on the island of Tenerife in 1492 did not permit Columbus to land on their island.

When Columbus and the Europeans who followed in his wake landed in the Americas, they were welcomed and initially worshiped as gods. The beardless Indians they encountered believed that the Spanish belonged to the same people as the legendary founders of their civilization, bearded men from across the Atlantic Ocean. According to the Aztec and Olmec (Central American Amerind) legends, their god, Quetzalcoatl, had Nordic features (eyes and hair color) and a beard. This god came from over the sea and taught the Amerinds how to raise corn and build structures.

There is indeed a marked similarity between the step pyramids to be found on the Canary Islands and those to be found in Central and South America, strongly suggesting yet another great lost White migration, this time to Central and South America, perhaps thousands of years before Columbus.

A red-haired mummy was also recovered from Nevado Ampato, Peru, near the famous Machu Picchu mountaintop fortress. The mummy was dated circa 1400 AD. It is not surprising that this date is 200 years after the Vikings left Europe for the Americas. "

When Cortez invaded Mexico City he was told that white men had been there centuries ago and that they said they would someday return. It is quite possible that those white men are the men that brought the starving Egyptians to this place, laid out and supervised the introduction of geoglyphs into the Mexican Pyramids and then departed, promising to return someday. It was the Mayans mistaken belief that the Spaniards were their friends returning as they had promised. That mistaken belief allowed the Spanish to enter Mexico City with little resistance and propagate misery and death on the peoples of Central and South America for centuries to come. (Read more about Cortez in the Chapter titled "Hernando Cortes, The Game Changer".)

END CHAPTER

Chapter 6

The Vikings

VIKING ORIGINS

No saga about the Americas would be complete without the story of the Vikings. Around 700 AD the Vikings simply appeared in the Baltic and North Sea. There did not seem to be a political or cultural evolution to the Viking story. Coincidentally, this is the same time period that the Galicians moved from their homeland of 700 years in Iberia to Denmark. The move was involuntary and was the result the collapse of the Roman Empire and an Arab invasion of Europe. When the Galicians, later to become the Danes, left Iberia they left their infrastructure behind. Prior to relocating, the Galicians were happy remaining in the background and letting the Roman government handle the politics and cost of defense while they reaped the harvest of government contracts and a protected mercantile.

As a result of the crumbling of the Roman Empire, by the time the Galicians moved from Iberia to Denmark they had lost both their government contracts and their protection. Now as Danes, they were faced with the prospect of the distrust of the Germans on one side and the hostility of the British on the other. Conditions and timing would indicate that the Galicians, now the Danes, made a pact with the Norsemen (Norway) to act as their military force. This would explain the Vikings sudden rise to power and their eventual conversion to Protestant Christianity. After all, the Celts were rich from their stay in Galicia and their mining operations in Cornwall England. They were also expert ship builders and had the expert Portuguese navigators to guide them.

It was shortly after the Vikings appearance that the Danes invaded and occupied Britain. The period of Danish occupation of Britain is known, to this day, as the period of Danelaw.

Norsemen

Norsemen is used to refer to the group of people as a whole who speak one of the North Germanic languages as their native language. ("Norse", in particular, refers to the Old Norse language belonging to the North Germanic branch of Indo-European languages, especially Norwegian, Icelandic, Swedish and Danish in their earlier forms.) The meaning of Norseman was "people from the North" and was applied primarily to Nordic people originating from southern and central Scandinavia. They established states and settlements in areas which today are part of the Faroe Islands, England, Scotland, Wales, Iceland, Finland, Ireland, Russia, Italy, Canada, Greenland, France, Ukraine, Estonia, Latvia, Lithuania, Germany and the USA.

The name Viking is applied to the People of Norway of the period from the late 8th century to the 11th century. The term "Normans" was later primarily associated with the people of Norse origin in Normandy, France, who later assimilated into French culture and language. The term Norse-Gaels was used concerning the people of Norse descent in Ireland and Scotland, who assimilated into the Gaelic culture.

WHO WERE THE VIKINGS?

A Viking is one of the Norse (Scandinavian) explorers, warriors, merchants, and pirates who raided and colonized wide areas of Europe from the late eighth to the early eleventh century. These Norsemen used their famed longships to travel as far east as Constantinople and the Volga River in Russia, and as far west as Iceland, Greenland, Newfoundland and Vineland, and later, having assimilated with the Celts, throughout Western North America. This period of Viking expansion is known as the Viking Age, and forms a major part of the medieval history of Scandinavia, the British Isles and Europe in general.

The period from the earliest recorded raids in the 790s until the Norman Conquest of England in 1066 is commonly known as the Viking Age of Scandinavian History. The Normans, however, were descended from Danish Vikings who were given feudal overlordship of areas in northern France — the Duchy of Normandy — in the 8th century. In that respect, descendants of the Vikings continued to have an influence in northern Europe. Likewise, King Harold Godwinson, the last Anglo-Saxon king of England who was killed during the Norman invasion in 1066, was descended from Danish Vikings. Many of the medieval kings of Norway and Denmark were married to English and Scottish royalty and Viking forces were often a factor in dynastic disputes prior to 1066.

Historically speaking, the Norwegians expanded to the north and west to places such as Ireland, Iceland and Greenland; the Danes to England and France, settling in the Danelaw (Northern England) Normandy, France; and Sweden to the east. These nations, although distinct, were similar in culture and language. The names of Scandinavian kings are known only for the later part of the Viking Age, and only after the end of the Viking Age did the separate kingdoms acquire a distinct identity as nations, which went hand in hand with their Christianization. Thus the end of the Viking Age for the Scandinavians also marks the start of their relatively brief Middle Ages.

VIKING SHIPS

There were two distinct classes of Viking ships: the longship (sometimes erroneously called "Drakkar", a corruption of "dragon" in Norse) and the "Knarr". The longship, intended for warfare and exploration, was designed for speed and agility, and was equipped with oars to complement the sail as well as making it able to navigate independently of the wind. The longship had a long and narrow hull, as well as a shallow draft, in order to facilitate landings and troop deployments in shallow water. The Knarr was a dedicated merchant vessel designed to carry cargo. It was designed with a broader hull, deeper draft and limited number of oars (used primarily to maneuver in harbors and similar situations). One Viking innovation was the beitass, a spar mounted to the sail that allowed their ships to sail effectively against the wind. This was a distinct advantage since their opponents had not yet learned this skill. All they had to do in order to escape another ship was to sail into the wind. While the Vikings maintained a relatively straight course their opponents would be required to zigzag.[26] Longships were used extensively by the Leidang, the Scandinavian defense fleets. The term "Viking ships" has entered common usage, however, possibly because of its romantic associations.

In Roskilde are the well-preserved remains of five ships, excavated from nearby Roskilde Fjord in the late 1960s. The ships were scuttled there in the

11th century to block a navigation channel, thus protecting the city, which was then the Danish capital, from seaborne assault. These five ships represent the two distinct classes of Viking ships, the Longship and the Knarr.

We know quite a bit about how the Vikings got to Vinland, thanks to archaeological discoveries of sunken ships and descriptions and drawings from the period. Only the very wealthy could afford the large ocean-going ships used in colonization and trade. Ships were either commissioned new from a master shipwright or purchased second-hand. There were no blueprints. Ship building was done 'by eye. Although the overall designs were similar, no ship was an exact replica of another. The smaller boats were, then as now, built locally where many people possessed boat building skills.

Viking ships were built from the outside in and from the bottom up. The keel was laid out first and the hull was built up from it. To hold the boards in shape as they were attached one by one, a "strongback" was erected over the construction site. The strongback was an overhead frame, anchored in the ground to which the hull was temporarily attached in the configuration desired.

Trees were selected specially for each boat or ship. The favored species were oak, pine, and spruce. Pieces that were to be angled in the ship were made from natural bends in the tree, for instance a piece cut from branches. The wood was not seasoned because the newly cut, "green" wood was more flexible. Steaming the boards made it easier to bend them into shape. The best boat boards were planks that had been cut radially from the trunk so that all planks included both the inner and outer portion of the trunk in the same proportions. This minimized the warping and shrinking as the wood dried, and it increased the tensile strength of the boards. Triangular in cross section, the boards were placed with their thinnest side placed downward, the thicker top overlapping the thin bottom part of the next plank. In big ships, planks had to be joined to produce the required length. This was done by 'scarfing,' that is the ends of the planks to be joined were thinned so that the end of one plank could overlap the other. After the hull was built up, "ribs" were inserted into it and attached to the hull with strong lashes of leather or even baleen from whales. This made the construction flexible so that the hull moved slightly with the water pressure rather than breaking from it.

The boards were held together with iron nails. The iron nails extended through both boards and through a rove over which they were tightly bent, "clenched," with hammer blows. The upper boards could also be attached with treenails. Treenails were dowels carved out of wood with an expanded head like a nail. Such treenails were also used in house construction and furniture. Steering was done with a large oar attached to the right hand side, "star board" ("steering board") side of the ship.

Most ships were stabilized with ballast of football-sized boulders which could be increased or discarded according to the weight of the cargo. The cargo ships also carried small open row boats which could be used for landing or loading and off-loading the ship.

Sails were large and rectangular, with a width of 10 meters or more and not quite as high as they were wide. They were made from lengths of wool, linen, or hemp sewn together as the widest piece of cloth one could produce on a loom of the era was 2 or 2.5 m. Most of us have seen the pictures of the Viking ships with the colorful striped sails. This color was achieved by sewing pirated wool, from captured Scotish ships, to their sails.

Because the ships were relatively light, they rode the crest of the waves rather than cutting through them. Travelling in these ships cannot have been too comfortable because they were largely open, like giant canoes. The cargo ships had a deck in the bow and could have one aft as well, but the rest of the ship was open. The crew and light goods were probably on the bow deck where they had cover in tarpaulins or tents. The heaviest cargo was stowed behind the mast. In addition to big ships there was a variety of smaller vessels of all sizes, both for rowing and sailing. Roads were poor, and the easiest way to transport people and goods was via waterways. Viking ships were sometimes referred to as "dragons." In Viking art, ships are often depicted with a dragon head atop the bow. One such carved head of wood has been found in the river Schelde in Belgium. It appears to have been removable.

Much of the inland areas traveled by the Norsemen cannot be accessed by ship today. By the end of the last ice age about 11,000 years ago, much of northern Europe and North America was covered by ice sheets up to 3 km thick. At the end of the ice age when the glaciers retreated, the removal of the weight from the depressed land led to a post-glacial rebound. Initially the rebound was rapid, proceeding at about 7.5 cm/year. This phase lasted for about 2,000 years, and took place as the ice was being unloaded. Once deglaciation was complete, uplift slowed to about 2.5 cm/year, and decreased exponentially after that. Today, typical uplift rates are of the order of 1 cm/year or less, and studies suggest that rebound will continue for about another 10,000 years. The total uplift from the end of deglaciation can be up to 400 m.

In Viking Age Malaren was still a bay of the Baltic Sea, and seagoing vessels could sail up it far into the interior of Sweden. Birka was conveniently near the trade routes through Sodertalje canal. Due to the post-glacial rebound, the Sodertalje canal and the mouth of Riddarfjarden bay had become so shallow by about 1200 that ships had to unload their cargoes near the entrances. After awhile the bay became a lake. The decline of Birka and the subsequent foundation of Stockholm at the choke point of Riddarfjarden were in part due to the post-glacial rebound changing the topography of the Malaren basin. The lake's surface currently averages 0.7 meters above sea level. Over time this post-glacial uplift caused many rivers and harbors, such as Bremen, Germany and Farum, Denmark, to be closed to boat trade.

NAVIGATION

Maps and Charts

Mariners relied on charts called "portolans" to assist them on their voyages. The portolans contained maps of coastlines, locations of harbors, river mouths, and manmade features visible from the sea. They were a compilation of centuries of seafarer observations. As sailors' skills improved and the use of the compass was more widespread, portolans improved in accuracy.

Portuguese chart makers added the meridian line, a point useful for latitude sailing as well as for navigating solely by compass. A geographic feature could now be located through the use of its distance in degree of latitude from a ship's point of departure.

The use of latitude and longitude was understood since before the time of Ptolemy in the second century A.D. He assigned coordinates to place names. However, the use of latitude and longitude posed difficulties while sailing on the high seas.

Early Navigation Methods

When a sailor departs port and loses sight of land, he must have some method of determining his direction. Early captains relied on nature to provide the answers. We all know the sun rises in the east and sets in the west. A rising sun on the left-hand side of the ship, for example, meant it was sailing south. At night, the pilot could view the Pole or North Star. This star does not change its position by the hour and it remains constant in the north. The farther north the sailor traveled, the higher the Pole Star appeared in the sky. The farther south he sailed, the lower the star appeared in the sky. When mariners reached the equator, the star disappeared. Navigators in the Southern Hemisphere were accustomed to using different stars to determine direction.

Determining latitude, the distance from north to south was measured by utilizing the Pole Star. Measuring the altitude of the star from the horizon and reading it in degrees was the same as the degrees of latitude above the equator. The quadrant, a quarter circle measuring 0 to 90 degrees marked around its curved edge, was a common instrument to assist in determining latitude. Its straight edges had tiny holes or sights on each end. A plumb line hung from the top. The navigator lined up the sights on the Pole Star and the plumb line would hang straight down over the curved area at a particular point. This would indicate the height of the star in degrees latitude.

Another way of determining latitude was with the use of the astrolabe. This was a simple wooden or brass disk with degrees marked around its edge. It had a rotating arm with small holes at either end. The disk would be hung vertically from a ring. The user could move the arm until the sunlight shone through the hole at one end and fell on the hole on the other end. The arm then would indicate the altitude by the degrees marked around the edge of the disk.

The drawback for both the quadrant and the astrolabe was the movement of the ship, which made it difficult to make an accurate measurement. The cross-staff, invented in the sixteenth century, solved this problem.

Determining longitude, the distance from east to west, was problematic. It is impossible to measure it without an accurate timepiece. (The chronometer was not invented until the eighteenth century.) For early sailors, the only way to measure it was to factor together variables of compass direction, speed, or dead reckoning. The compass was well known to Europeans in the fifteenth century. It had been used in China and Arabia centuries before. Compasses of the fifteenth century were made with an iron needle magnetized by a lodestone on a small piece of wood floating in a container of water. This was eventually replaced by a brass canister where a magnetic needle swung around an upright pin. The compass was not always accurate because magnetic north is not the same as true north.

Another method of navigating open sea was the complicated process of dead reckoning. The pilot had to estimate the ship's speed with a chip log, which had a weighted wooden float attached to a line with knots in it. This line would be thrown from the stern. Time was measured with one-minute glasses. The number of knots pulled off the reel by the drifting log determined speed. This information combined with the known direction of the compass would determine progress along longitudinal lines. Time, distance, and direction were measured each time the ship changed tack due to wind direction. This zigzag plotting was calculated with a traverse board.

Celtic Navigation

The ancient Norsemen knew of all the methods outlined above. However, they had one more navigation advantage which they used and kept secret. The Norse knew about Magnetic Deviation. Magnetic Deviation plays a part in any plan to use a magnetic compass to traverse the Earth. Anywhere on earth there is spurious magnetism that affects the accuracy of a compass. This magnetic error is different, although relatively constant, anywhere on the earth. If you were to use your compass alone to make a long trip you would wind up many miles from your intended destination. The Nordics had knowledge of this anomaly and had charted the amount of error that existed anywhere on earth. In this manner they could adjust their compass for the error and sail precisely to their destination with a very small margin of error. This knowledge is demonstrated in the next Plate, and in the Chapter titled "The Newport Tower and The Kensington Runestone", which shows that the both the Northwest and Northeast corners of what would become the United States and Canadian border both terminate at points that display exactly 20 degrees of magnetic deviation. Another method available to ancient mariners was Celestial navigation. Celestial Navigation is not affected by Magnetic Deviation and provides a true course from point A to point B. The problem with using celestial navigation aboard ship is it is difficult to obtain an accurate reading due to the motion of the ship and cloud cover. Our modern version of this true course navigation is called GPS. The Vikings also made use of an opaque stone through which they could see the position of the sun during overcast days.

DECLINE

Following a period of thriving trade and Viking settlement, cultural impulses flowed from the rest of Europe to affect Viking dominance. Christianity had an early and growing presence in Scandinavia, and with the rise of a centralized authority and the creation of the Baltic trade organization known as the Hansiatic League, Viking raids became more risky and less profitable.

A new quasi-feudalistic system became entrenched in Scandinavian rule and, as a result, organized opposition sealed the Vikings' fate. Eleventh-century chronicles note Scandinavian attempts to combat the Vikings from the eastern shores of the Baltic Sea. Upon the Vikings departure the Danish and Swedish participated in the Baltic Crusades during the 12th and 13th centuries. This was a prelude to the development of the **Hanseatic League**, a Baltic trade organization that did not want piracy to interfere with there trade in the Baltic Sea.

One of the primary profit centers of Viking trade was slavery. The Protestant Christian Church took a position that Christians should not own other humans as slaves, so chattel slavery diminished as a practice throughout Northern Europe. Eventually, outright slavery was outlawed, replaced with serfdom at the bottom rung of Medieval society. This took much of the economic incentive out of raiding, though sporadic activity continued for a few decades beyond the Norman conquest of England. This anti-slavery belief was carried over to the newly established United States by it's founding fathers.

CULTURAL LEGACY

In England, the Viking Age began dramatically on June 8, 793 when Norsemen destroyed the abbey on the island of Lindisfarne. The devastation of Northumbria's Holy Island shocked and alerted the Royal Courts of Europe to the Viking presence. "Never before has such an atrocity been seen," declared the Northumbrian scholar, Alcuin of York. More than any other single event, the attack on Lindisfarne demonized perception of the

Vikings for the next twelve centuries. Not until the 1890s did scholars outside Scandinavia begin to seriously reassess the achievements of the Vikings, recognizing their artistry, technological skills and seamanship.

The first challenges to anti-Viking sentiments in Britain emerged in the 17th century. Pioneering scholarly editions of the Viking Age began to reach a small readership in Britain, archaeologists began to dig up Britain's Viking past, and linguistic enthusiasts started to identify the Viking-Age origins for rural idioms and proverbs. The new dictionaries of the Old Norse language enabled the Victorians to grapple with the primary Icelandic sagas.

In Scandinavia, the 17th century Danish scholars Thomas Bartholin and Ole Worm, and Olof Rudbeck of Sweden were the first to set the standard for using runic inscriptions and Icelandic Sagas as historical sources. During the Age of Enlightenment and the Nordic Renaissance, historical scholarship in Scandinavia became more rational and pragmatic, as witnessed by the works of a Danish historian Ludvig Holberg and Swedish historian Olof von Dalin.

Until recently, the history of the Viking Age was largely based on Icelandic sagas, the history of the Danes written by Saxo Grammaticus, the Russian Primary Chronicle and the War of the Irish with the Foreigners. Although few scholars still accept these texts as reliable sources, historians nowadays rely more on archeology and numismatics, disciplines that have made valuable contributions toward understanding the period.

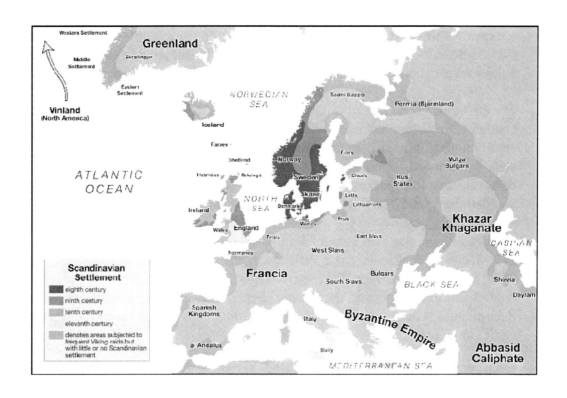

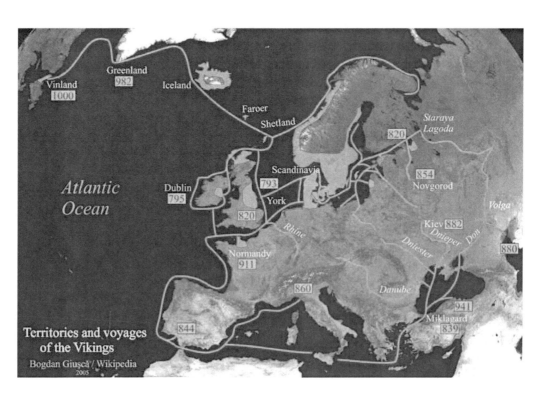

Territories and voyages
of the Vikings
Bogdan Giuşcă / Wikipedia
2005

After 1066 the Viking Role in European History came to a close. However, the Celts and their allies had a secret knowledge of the geography of the world. As you read on evidence will show that the Vikings moved on to colonize vast areas of North America. As will unfold in the following chapters, the Danes and Vikings had enjoyed millennia of free and secret access to the Americas. With the increasing amount of exploration by the countries of Europe it was inevitable that their colonies, mining and timber resources, in the Americas would be discovered. It was now the Vikings role to survey, and colonize the Americas before the European masses arrived. Is it realistic to believe that the Vikings explored the entire known world but had no desire to explore further South than Newfoundland?

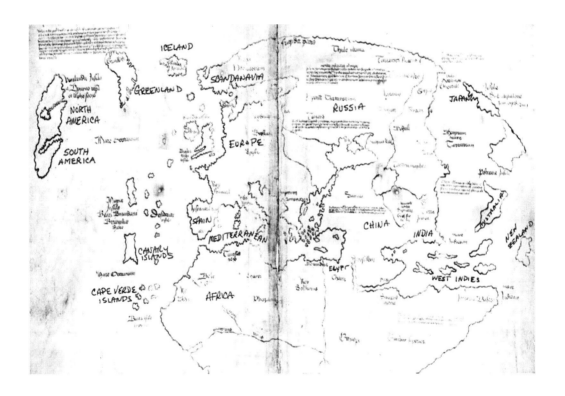

Norse Map Circa 1450AD

If this map is studied closely it soon becomes obvious that the map contains a map of the entire world, including North and South America. It is simply out of proportion to the rest of the map. The map clearly shows Canada, the Saint Lawrence Seaway leading into the Great Lakes, Florida, the Gulf of Mexico and South America.

In the next chapter you will be introduced to a geoglyph outlining the territory allocated to the Vikings, by the Celtic Alliance, in which they were to settle, and protect North America from Europeans, until they were assimilated into the future cultures of the New World.

END CHAPTER

Chapter 7

The Vikings in the Americas

GREENLAND

The Norse colonization of the Americas began as early as the 10th century AD, when Norse sailors (often referred to as Vikings) explored and settled areas of the North Atlantic, including the northeastern portions of North America along the East Coast.

According to the Sagas of Icelanders, Norsemen from Iceland first settled Greenland in the 980s. There is no reason to doubt the authority of the information that the sagas supply regarding the very beginning of the settlement, but it should be noted nonetheless that because they embody the literary preoccupations of writers and audiences in medieval Iceland they are not always reliable.

Erik the Red (Old Norse: Eiríkr rauði), having been banished from Iceland for manslaughter, is said to have explored the uninhabited southwestern coast of Greenland during the three years of his banishment. He made plans to entice settlers to the area, even purposefully choosing the name Greenland to attract potential colonists, saying "that people would be more eager to go there because the land had a good name". The inner reaches of one long fjord, named Eiriksfjord after him, was where he eventually established his estate Brattahlid and issued tracts of land to his followers.

VINLAND AND L'ANSE AUX MEADOWS

According to the Icelandic sagas ("Eirik the Red's Saga" and the "Saga of the Greenlanders"—chapters of the Hauksbók and the Flatey Book), the Norse started to explore lands to the west of Greenland only a few years after the Greenland settlements were established. In 985 while sailing from Iceland to Greenland with a migration fleet consisting of 400-700 settlers and 25 other ships (14 of which completed the journey), a merchant named Bjarni Herjolfsson was blown off course and after three days sailing he sighted land west of the fleet. Bjarni was only interested in finding his father's farm, but he did describe his discovery to Leif Ericson who explored the area in more detail and built a small settlement fifteen years later.

The sagas describe three separate areas discovered during this exploration: Helluland, which means "land of the flat stones" (Possibly Labrador); Markland, "the land of forests", (Possibly Canada and New England) definitely of interest to settlers in Greenland where there were few trees; and Vinland, "the land of wine", (Possibly Martha's Vineyard and Rhode Island) found somewhere south of Markland. Many Early Nordic relics have been found in the Rhode Island area. (See below) It was in Vinland that the settlement, described in the sagas, was built. Credence is further given to Rhode Island as the location of Vineland since there exists the 7000 year old Egyptian geoglyph, named the Gulfo de Cintra geoglyph, that points to the enigmatic City of Newport, Rhode Island, USA, with it's now famous Newport Tower. (See the chapter titled "The Newport Tower and the Kensington Runestone".) As will be documented later in this chapter there is evidence that the Viking territory included Rhode Island and the mysterious city of Newport.

Evidence of Norse voyages to the New England area continue to be discovered. This includes the Maine Penny, a Norwegian coin from King Olaf Kyrre's reign (1066-80) allegedly found in a Native American archaeological site in the U.S. state of Maine, suggesting an exchange between the Norse and the Native Americans late in or after the 11th century; and an entry in the Icelandic Annals from 1347 which refers to a small Greenlandic vessel with a crew of eighteen that arrived in Iceland while attempting to return to Greenland from Markland with a load of timber. In addition, Norse materials have been excavated in several Inuit communities. Then there are the scores of Nordic Runestones that have been found, and are being found on a regular basis, that cover the Eastern portion of the North American landscape, from Canada to Texas.

THE VIKING GEOGLYPH

Scholars have been debating for centuries as to how far south, in North America, the Viking exploration covered. After you finish this book it is hoped that you will have grasped the idea that the Egyptians, as well as the Celtic Danes/Galicians who sponsored the Vikings, visited most of North and South America long before and after the Vikings. As has been the case with every major culture which we have researched, the Vikings have left us a signpost which outlines what they considered their territory. Although there are many Viking relics being found all over the Central and Eastern parts of North America there is one indisputable geoglyph which they left behind that should answer everyone's question as to how far south the Vikings traveled in their early explorations. That is the Tiniteqilaq, Greenland geoglyph depicted below. The glyph is well hidden in the Sermilk fjord in Eastern Greenland and is a prime example of the value of this new science called Geoglyphology. It is possible, since this territory lies entirely within the Celtic Territory outlined by Stonehenge, that the Vikings were given this territory by the Celts when the Vikings left the North Sea area c1000 AD. It becomes obvious from the Viking relics found outside this area that the Viking area of exploration was not contained within these boundaries.

**The Tiniteqilaq Geoglyph (65 53 23.72N 37 46 24.91W),
located on the Sermilk fjord, Greenland**

Radials generated by the North half of the Tiniteqilaq geoglyph.

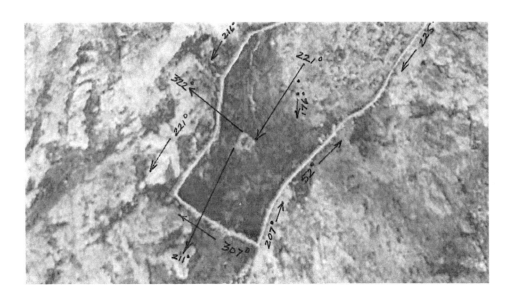

Radials generated by the South half of the Tiniteqilaq geoglyph.

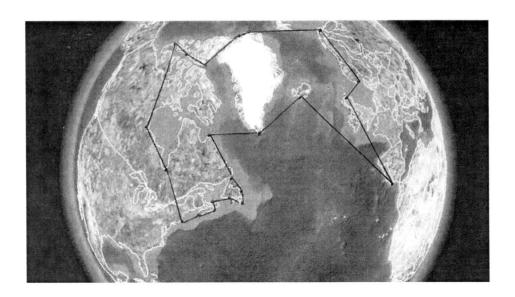

**The boundaries of the early Viking Territory as described
in the Tiniteqilaq, Greenland geoglyph.**

After researching ancient European history, and correlating that with the various associated geoglyphs, the boundaries depicted above fit perfectly within the Giza Pyramid 045 degree boundaries emanating from Baja

113

California and the tip of South America, minus the following; Wales, Cornwall, Brittany, the Netherlands, Denmark, Eastern England and Scotland. The previously described countries that are missing from the Viking map, but lay West of the Giza 045 degree radial, are precisely the territory in which the Galicians, later to become the Danes, and their allies occupied shortly before the Vikings disappeared from the history books circa 1100 AD. The evidence suggests that the Vikings were part of the North Sea Alliance, and after their assistance in protecting Celtic interests in Western Europe, were given the portion of the territory, described by the Stonehenge geoglyph, in which to live in safety and protect Celtic interests in North America. Coincidently, this is precisely the same period in which the dating of Viking relics in North America indicate that they begin their explorations there. In short, when the Vikings suddenly disappeared from Europe circa 1100 AD it appears that they moved to, and colonized, the territory depicted in the Tiniteqilaq geoglyph. This is not to say that they did not venture further into North America later.

NORDIC MOORING STONES IN NEWPORT, RI

The following Mooring Stones were found on the West coast of Newport Island, RI USA. Until now these have only been known in locations where early Nordic mariners were known to have traveled, Minnesota, Saint Lawrence Seaway, etc.. These stones were used to moor Nordic Ships in the 11th and 12th century. It looks like the theory that the Vikings only traveled as far south as Nova Scotia is slowly sinking into Narragansett Bay. (These Mooring Stones were discovered by Peter and Steve DiMarzo, Newport, RI USA)

The Typical Triangular Hole

A Mooring Stone With a Hole in the Top

Mooring Stones in the Sunset

A TERRITORIAL CHRONOLOGY

I am hoping that what you are about to read will astound and educate. In a nutshell, what follows is what this book is all about. What you are about to read is a chronology of territories which by all indications were established over 10,000 years ago and whose impact has carried down to this very day. Our next book will contain the many other territories that we are currently researching, around the world. This information fills in the many gaps that have existed in the history books and answers questions which inquiring people have been asking for centuries. As you will notice the original territories do not overlap and show a concentrated effort to describe three territories, for whom, and for what reasons we do not yet know. As validation of the original territories you will see below that the master artist Diego Rivera secretly included these same geoglyphical boundaries in his painting titled "Michoacan". The boundaries which Diego projects in his painting encompass all of the territories outlined in the Stonehenge, Inspiration Peak and Caral Geoglyphs.

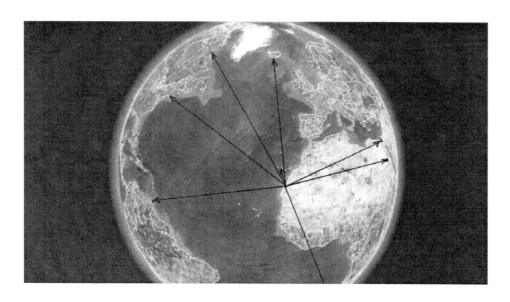

Gulfo de Cintra, Africa - Egyptian Territory

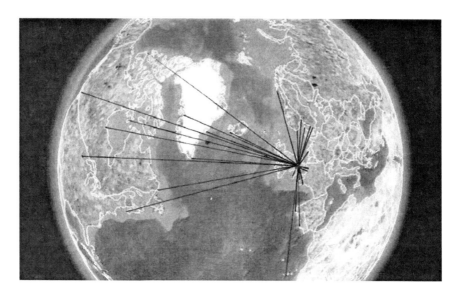

Stonehenge, UK - The Celtic Territory

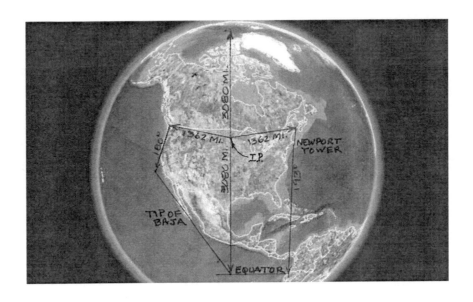

Inspiration Peak, Minnesota USA - The North American Territory

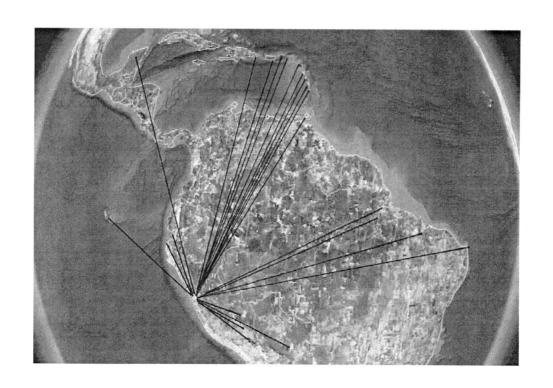

Caral, Peru - The South American Territory

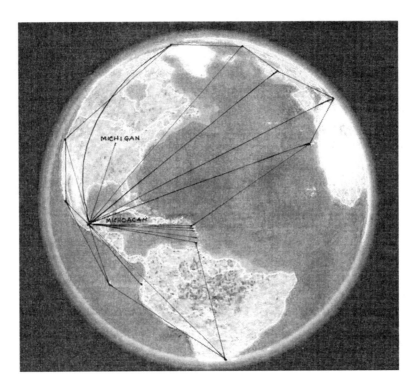

The Diego Rivera Mural "Michoacan" Boundaries

There is another, mathematical, factor that ties the Celtic, North American and South American territorial geoglyphs together. They all have the number 22.7 in common. On the Stonehenge 090 degree radial, at 22.7 miles, is a significant geoglyph. Remember that in ancient times 090 was the direction in which all maps were oriented. Circling the Inspiration Peak Survey Marker at 22.7 miles, at each 10 degree increment, is a circular geoglyph. In addition, the large circular geoglyph that was identified in the South American territorial geoglyph is 22.7 miles across. (See the next three photos below.)

The 090 Degree Marker at 22.7 Miles from Stonehenge

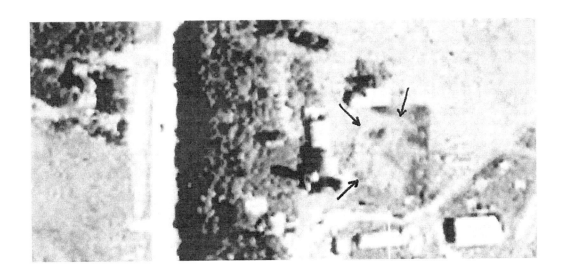

The 360 Degree Marker at 22.7 Miles from Inspiration Peak

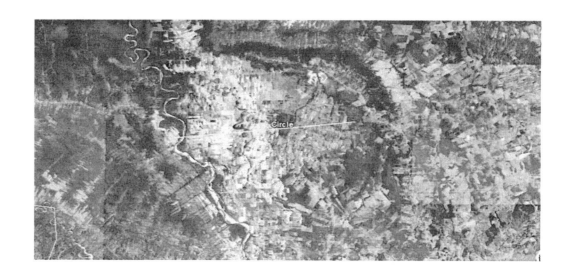

The 22.7 mile wide South American Circle Glyph

The following photos show territorial boundaries that were developed after, but lie within, the original four territories

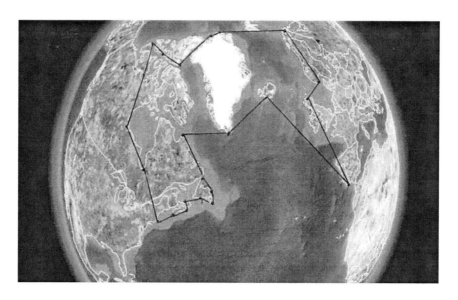

Tiniteqilaq, Greenland - The Viking Territory - Circa 1100 AD

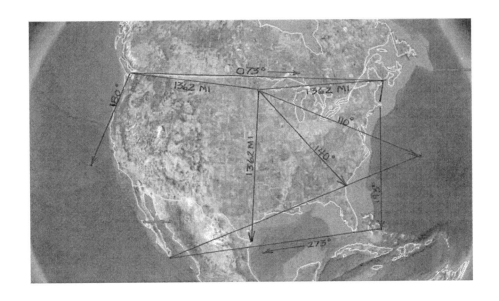

**Inspiration Peak, USA - Revised North American Territory –
Circa 1559 AD After the Spanish Conquest of Mexico in 1519.**

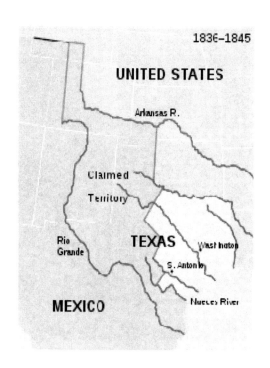

Mexican Territorial Claim - 1845 AD

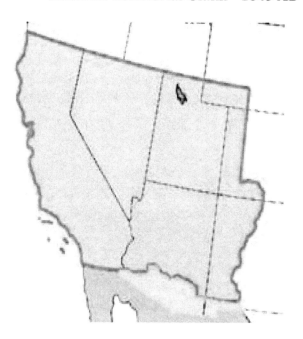

**Mexican Land Ceded to the US in 1848 AD by "The Treaty of Hidalgo"
after the war with Mexico.**

VIKING LANDMARKS IN AMERICA

Many Nordic runestones and relics have been found in the United States, most dating around the 11th and 12th Century. Scholars have argued up to now that they were most likely fakes. However, there are so many of them being found now, from Maine to Texas, that argument just doesn't hold water any longer. A runestone is typically a raised stone with a runic inscription, but the term can also be applied to inscriptions on boulders and on bedrock. The tradition began in the 4th century, and it lasted into the 12th century, but most of the runestones date from the late Viking Age. Most runestones are located in Scandinavia, but there are also scattered runestones in locations that were visited by Norsemen during the Viking Age. Ref: Keyword "runestone" - http://www.wikipedia.com .

END CHAPTER

Chapter 8

The Mississippians

Locations of the Mississippian Tribes

MISSISSIPPIAN CULTURE

The Mississippian culture was a mound-building Native American culture that flourished in what are now the Midwestern, Eastern, and Southeastern United States from approximately 800 AD to 1500 AD, varying regionally. The Mississippian way of life began to develop in the Mississippi River Valley (for which it is named). Cultures in the tributary Tennessee River Valley may have also begun to develop Mississippian characteristics at this point. Almost all dated Mississippian sites predate 1500 AD, which coincides with the time that the Spanish Explorers begin their reign of genocide in the Americas. Could the explorers have brought disease to the area or was conquest their objective. Based on Spanish orders, about this time, Panfilo de Narvaez was charged with establishing colonies along the Gulf Coast of what is now the United States. History has recorded many battles between the indigenous peoples and the Spanish in the Southeast portion of North America.

CULTURAL TRAITS

A number of cultural traits are recognized as being characteristic of the Mississippians. Although not all Mississippian peoples practiced all of the following activities, they were distinct from other tribes in adoption of some or all of these traits:

1. The construction of large, truncated earthwork pyramid mounds, or platform mounds.
Such mounds were usually square, rectangular, or occasionally circular. Structures (domestic houses, temples, burial buildings, or other) were usually constructed atop such mounds. (Sounds like Egyptian influence.)

2. Maize-based agriculture.
In most places, the development of Mississippian culture coincided with adoption of comparatively large-scale, intensive maize agriculture, which allowed support of larger populations and craft specialization. Although maize was unknown in Europe at the time, maize is a common decoration on the 15th century Rosslyn Chapel built in Scotland to honor the Templers. The Templers supposedly disappeared in the 14th century. It is more likely

they came to North America. There are stories of Templers assisting the Scots in winning their freedom over England in the 14th Century.

3. The adoption and use of riverine (or more rarely marine) shell-tempering agents in their ceramics.
Shell tempering agents were also found in the mortar of the Newport Tower.

4. Widespread trade networks extending as far west as the Rockies, North to the Great Lakes, South to the Gulf of Mexico, and East to the Atlantic Ocean.

5. The development of the chiefdom or complex chiefdom level of social complexity.

6. The development of institutionalized social inequality.

This differs from the Western Indian practice of equality and sharing. It does however conform to a European influence.

7. A centralization of control of combined political and religious power in the hands of a few.

8. The beginnings of a settlement hierarchy.
In this hierarchy one major center (with mounds) has clear influence or control over a number of lesser communities, which may or may not possess a smaller number of mounds.

9. The adoption of the paraphernalia of the Southeastern Ceremonial Complex (SECC) also called the Southern Cult.

This is the belief system of the Mississippians as we know it. SECC items are found in Mississippian-culture sites from Wisconsin (see Aztalan State Park) to the Gulf Coast, and from Florida to Arkansas and Oklahoma. The SECC was frequently tied in to ritual game-playing.

CHRONOLOGY

The Mississippian stage is usually divided into three or more periods. Each of these periods is an arbitrary historical distinction that varies from region to region. At one site, each period may be considered to begin earlier or later, depending on the speed of adoption or development of given Mississippian traits.

Early Mississippian cultures are those which had just made the transition from the Late Woodland period way of life (500–1000 AD). Different groups abandoned tribal life ways for increasing complexity, sedentism, centralization, and agriculture. The Early Mississippian period is considered to be, in most places, c. 1000–1200 AD (The same time period that the Vikings were said to have come to North America.) The production of surplus corn and attractions of the regional chiefdoms both led to rapid concentrations of population in major centers.

The Middle Mississippian period is often considered the high point of the Mississippian era. The expansion of the great metropolis and ceremonial complex at Cahokia, the formation of other complex chiefdoms, and the spread and development of SECC art and symbolism are characteristic changes of this period. The Mississippian traits listed above came to be widespread throughout the region. In most places, this period is recognized as occurring c. 1200–1400 C.E.

The Late Mississippian period, usually considered circa 1400 to European contact, is characterized by increasing warfare, political turmoil, and population movement. The population of Cahokia dispersed early in this period (circa 1400), perhaps migrating to other rising political centers. More defensive structures are often seen at sites, and sometimes a decline in mound-building and ceremonialism. Although some areas continued an essentially Middle Mississippian culture until the first significant contact with Europeans, the population of most areas had dispersed or were experiencing severe social stress by 1500. As will be discussed later, this period coincides with the opening of the Portuguese Navigation School in 1419. This would have been the beginning of the exploration and conquest of the New World by factions other than the Orthodox Christians and Egyptians, who had befriended the natives of the Americas.

FIRST RECORDED CONTACT WITH EUROPEANS

The Hernando de Soto expedition, through the Southeast, reported Native Americans of the Mississippian culture interacted with Spanish explorers of the Juan Pardo expedition. Juan Pardo built a base in South Carolina in 1567 called Fort San Juan. Expedition documentation and archaeological evidence of the fort and Native American culture both exist. The soldiers were at the fort about 18 months (1567-1568) before the natives killed them and destroyed the fort. They killed soldiers stationed at five other forts as well; only one man of 120 survived. Sixteenth-century Spanish artifacts have been recovered from the site, marking the first "recorded" European colonization in the interior of what became the United States.

Scholars have searched the records of Hernando de Soto in 1539–1543 looking for evidence of contacts with Mississippians. He visited many villages, in some cases staying for a month or longer. Some encounters were violent, while others were relatively peaceable. In some cases, de Soto seems to have been used as a tool or ally in long-standing native feuds. In one example, de Soto negotiated a truce between the Pacaha and the Casqui.

De Soto's later encounters left about half of the Spaniards and perhaps many hundreds of Native Americans dead. The chronicles of de Soto are among the first documents written about Mississippian peoples, and are an invaluable source of information on their cultural practices. The chronicles of the Narvaez Expedition was written before the de Soto expedition; in fact, it was the Narvaez expedition (1527) that informed the Court of de Soto about the New World. Curiously Narvaez was among the first Europeans to have contact with the Mississippians. This occurred at the very end of the Mississippian divination. If the Spanish were the first to contact the Native Americans one would have to ask; How did all the Nordic artifacts found at Mississippian sites arrive there centuries before?

After the destruction and flight of the de Soto expedition, the Mississippian peoples continued their way of life with little direct European influence. Indirectly, however, European introductions would change the face of Eastern North America. Diseases such as measles and smallpox caused so many fatalities, because the natives lacked immunity, that they undermined the social order of many chiefdoms. Some groups adopted European horses and changed back to nomadism. Political structures collapsed in many places. By the time more documentary evidence was being written, the Mississippian way of life had changed irrevocably. Some groups maintained an oral tradition link to their mound-building past. Other Native American groups, having migrated many hundreds of miles and having lost their elders to diseases, did not know their ancestors had built the mounds dotting the landscape.

SPIRO MOUNDS, OKLAHOMA

Spiro Mounds is one of the most important pre-Columbian archaeological sites in the United States. Located in Eastern Oklahoma near the modern town of Spiro, it is under the protection of the Oklahoma Historical Society and open to the public. It is listed on the National Register of Historic Places.

Spiro is the western-most known outpost of the Mississippian culture that arose and spread along the lower Mississippi River and its tributaries between the 800s and 1500s AD. As in other Mississippian-culture towns, the people built a number of large, complex earthworks. These included earthen mounds surrounding a large, planned and leveled central plaza, where important religious rituals, the politically and culturally significant game of chunkey, and other important community activities were carried out. The population lived in a village that bordered the plaza. In addition, archaeologists have found more than twenty other related village sites within five miles of the main town. Other village sites linked to Spiro through culture and trade have been found up to a hundred miles away.

Spiro was inhabited between about 950 and 1450 CE. (Once again, the demise of the Mississippian culture coincides with the later European exploration of the Americas.) It was the headquarters town of a regional chiefdom, whose powerful leaders directed the building of eleven platform mounds and one burial mound in an 80-acre (0.32 km2) area on the south bank of the Arkansas River. The heart of the site is a group of nine mounds surrounding an oval plaza. These mounds elevated the homes of important leaders or formed the foundations for religious structures that focused the attention of the community. Brown Mound, the largest platform mound, is located on the eastern side of the plaza. It had an earthen ramp that gave access to the summit from the north side. Here, atop Brown Mound and the other mounds, the town's inhabitants carried out complex rituals, centered especially on the deaths and burials of Spiro's powerful rulers.

Archaeologists have shown that Spiro had a large resident population until about 1250 CE. After that, most of the population moved to other towns nearby. Spiro continued to be used as a regional ceremonial center and burial ground until about 1450 CE. Its ceremonial and mortuary functions continued and seem to have grown after the main population moved away.

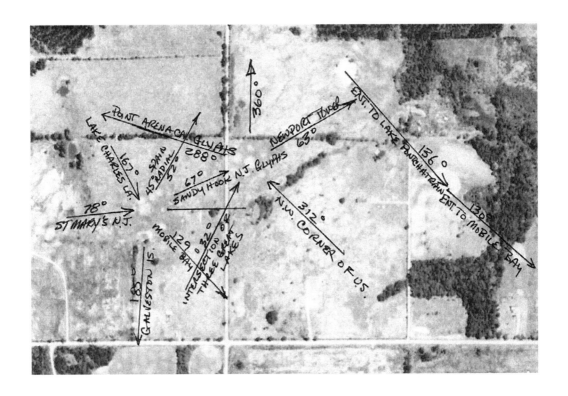

Spiro Mounds, Oklahoma Glyph With Associated Radials

As is common with most Mississippian Mound geoglyphs, the endpoints of these radials all coincide with the future boundaries of the United States. This would indicate a coordinated effort by the builders of the mounds to define a territory that they considered their own.

MOUNDVILLE, ALABAMA

Moundville Archaeological Site, also known as the Alabama Archaeological Park, is a Mississippian site on the Black Warrior River in Hale County, near the town of Moundville. Extensive archaeological investigation has shown that the site was the political and ceremonial center of a regionally organized Mississippian culture chiefdom polity between the 11th and 15th centuries. The archaeological park portion of the site is administered by the University of Alabama Museums and encompasses 172 acres (70 ha), consisting of 32 platform mounds around a rectangular plaza. The site was declared a

National Historic Landmark in 1964 and was added to the National Register of Historic Places in 1966.

Moundville is the second-largest site of the classic Middle Mississippian era (after Cahokia in Illinois). The culture was expressed in villages and chiefdoms throughout the central Mississippi River Valley, the lower Ohio River Valley, and most of the Mid-South area, including Kentucky, Tennessee, Alabama, and Mississippi as the core of the classic Mississippian culture area.

The site was occupied from around 1120 CE to 1450 CE. The community took the form of a 300-acre (121 ha) residential and political area protected on three sides by a bastioned wooden palisade wall, with the remaining side protected by the river bluff. (The Celts were known for centuries for their wooden forts.) The largest platform mounds are located on the northern edge of the plaza and become increasingly smaller going either clockwise or counter clockwise around the plaza to the south. Scholars theorize that the highest-ranking clans occupied the large northern mounds with the smaller mounds' supporting buildings used for residences, mortuary, and other purposes. Of the two largest mounds in the group, Mound A occupies a central position in the great plaza, and Mound B lies just to the north, a steep, 58 feet (18 m) tall pyramidal mound with two access ramps. The description sounds very similar to the Pyramids of Mexico.

Archaeologists have interpreted this community plan as a sociogram, an architectural depiction of a social order based on ranked clans. According to this model, the Moundville community was segmented into a variety of different clan precincts, the ranked position of which was represented in the size and arrangement of paired earthen mounds around the central plaza. By 1300 the site was being used more as a religious and political center than as a residential town. This signaled the beginning of a decline, and by 1500 most of the area was abandoned.

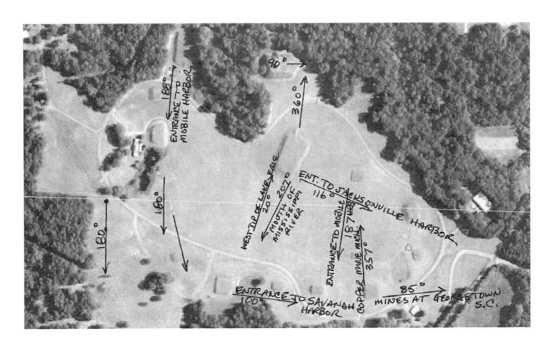

Moundville, AL Geoglyph 1

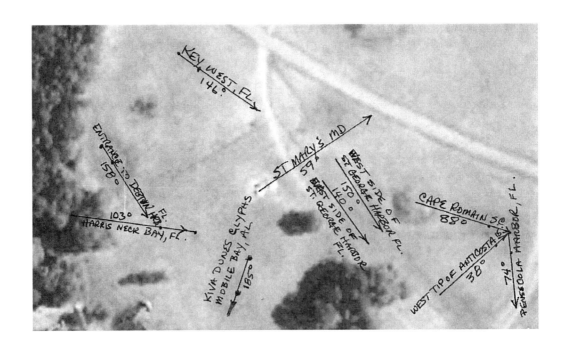

Moundville, AL Geoglyph 2

**All Seeing Eye, Circa 1200 AD. Found at Moundville, AL.
This is the same symbol found on our one dollar bill and
in Egyptian history.**

Mississippian Pottery. Notice the Viking Sail Stripes and Colors on the left vase and the Red Saint George Cross on the Right Vase.

THE NEWARK DECALOGUE STONE

The Newark Holy Stones are a set of artifacts discovered by David Wyrick, a land surveyor, in 1860 within a cluster of ancient Indian burial mounds near Newark, Ohio. The artifact was unearthed from under tons of earth covering an ancient burial mound, under the supervision of nine witnesses. Hardly the work of someone playing a hoax. The set consists of the Keystone, a stone bowl, and the Decalogue, with its sandstone box. They can be viewed at the Johnson-Humrickhouse Museum in Coshocton, Ohio. The site where the objects were found is known as The Newark Earthworks, one of the biggest collections from an ancient American Indian culture, known as the Hopewell Indians. The Hopewell Culture existed from approximately 100 BC to AD 500. That does not necessarily mean that the burial mound was constructed that early.

136

The Stone

Unlike other ancient artifacts found previously in this region, the Keystone was inscribed with Hebrew. It contains one phrase on each side:

Holy of Holies
King of the Earth
The Law of God
The Word of God

The Decalogue Limestone Box with Stone

Back of Stone

Photos courtesy of J. Houston McCulloch

The stone is carved with post-Exilic square Hebrew letters on all sides translated to be a condensed version of the Ten Commandments. The name Decalogue Stone, comes from the translation of the Hebrew letters that outline the religious and moral codes described in Exodus 20:2-17 and Deuteronomy 5:6-21, which refer to the Decalogue or Ten Commandments. The inscription begins on the front at the top of an arch above the figure of a bearded man who is wearing a turban, robe, and appears to be holding a tablet. It runs down the left side, continues around all sides, and makes its way back to the front up the right side to where it began. This pattern indicates that the inscription was meant to be read repetitively. Right above the figure of the man is a separate inscription which translates to "Moses". Also found nearby during the same excavation was a small stone bowl about the size of a tea cup, which is also on display with the other artifacts.

If it is difficult to believe that there are Hebrew relics in the Americas don't forget that the Christians were Hebrew before their conversion. Hence an Old and New Testament in the Bible. The Hebrews did not distance themselves from their Christian Brothers, but in fact they worked and fought together. A good example is the sack of Rome in 400AD. Research has shown that the colonists of the 10th thru the 14th Centuries AD were both Christian and Hebrew. As you can see the duration of the Mississippians, throughout Eastern North America was primarily from 1000 AD to 1500 AD. This is precisely the period between when the Vikings established colonies in America. It is entirely possible that these people were Egyptians relocated earlier to colonize the Americas which were being visited and influenced by the Vikings and their successors.

THE POVERTY POINT GEOGLYPH

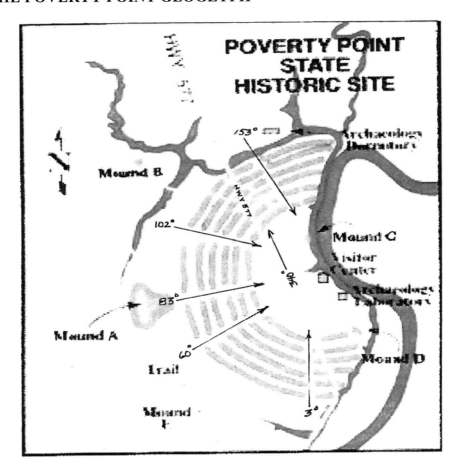

The Poverty Point Glyph, LA, USA

END POINTS FOR THE RADIALS IN THE ABOVE PHOTO

003 Degree Radial - True North
060 Degree Radial - The Geoglyph at Cape May, NJ

083 Degree Radial - Bermuda Island
102 Degree Radial - Amelia Island
153 Degree Radial - Entrance to the Mississippi River

Poverty Point State Historic Site

Eight centuries after Egyptian slaves drug huge stones across the desert to build the Great Pyramids, and before the great Mayan pyramids were constructed the Poverty Point inhabitants set for themselves an enormous task as they built a complex array of earthen mounds and ridges overlooking the Mississippi River flood plain in what is now northeastern Louisiana. - U.S. National Park Service. 8/26/2009

Poverty Point comprises several earthworks and mounds built between 1650 and 700 BCE, during the Archaic period in the Americas by a group of Native Americans of the Poverty Point culture. The culture extended 100 miles (160 km) across the Mississippi Delta. The original purposes of Poverty Point have not been determined by archaeologists, although they have proposed various possibilities including that it was: a settlement, a trading center, and/or a ceremonial religious complex.

The site, which has been described as "the largest and most complex Late Archaic earthwork occupation and ceremonial site yet found in North America" is a registered National Monument. The monument was brought to the attention of archaeologists in the early 20th century, when it was given the name of Poverty Point after a nearby plantation. Since then, various excavations have taken place at the site, and various theories have been suggested regarding its purpose, which range from the archaeological to the pseudo-archaeological and the New Age, while it has remained as a tourist attraction. - Wikipedia

The Poverty Point site fits nicely into an extensive collection of Eastern and Central American tribes known collectively as the Mississippians. Research has shown that these tribes had extensive contact with pre-Columbian Europeans. Not surprisingly these tribes were mound (dirt pyramid) builders. In the diagram below you will see confirmation of a continuity of thought between the 6500 year old Poverty Point culture and the 600 year old pre-Columbian European culture.

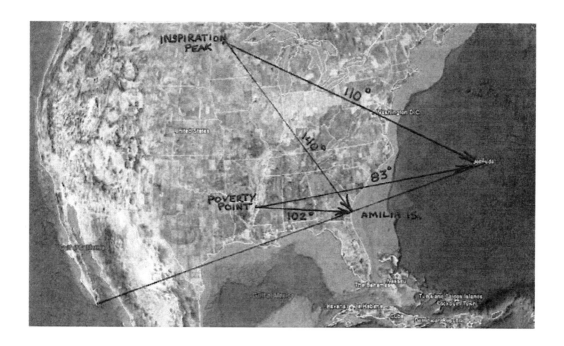

The Poverty Point Connection

As you can see two of the radials emanating from the Poverty Point Geoglyph (c4500 BC) define two of the same points that were identified in the Kensington Runestone (c1472 AD) instructions referencing Inspiration Peak. What are the chances that a 6500 year old culture would even use the same methodology as a 600 year old culture. Add on top of that the chances of them both identifying the same two important points, in a land claim thousands of miles away, is astronomical. This type of verification is not atypical. Our Foundation has discovered and proven this same continuity worldwide. The oldest geoglyphs containing these same characteristics are 10,000 years old.

WEBER FALLS, OKLAHOMA

Weber Falls, Oklahoma has been officially recorded as the home of one of the Mississippian Indian tribes. However, the identification of pottery bearing Viking and Templar insignias and the presence of ancient geoglyphs calls into question the ethnicity of the Mississippian Tribes.

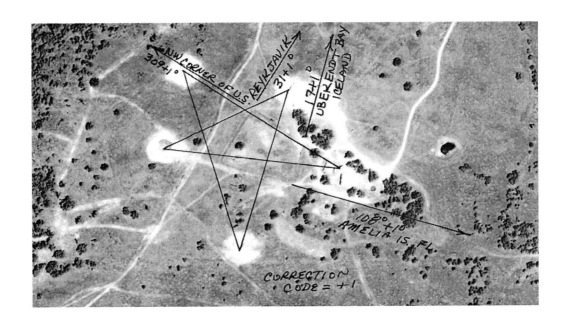

One of the Weber Falls, Oklahoma Geoglyphs

This geoglyph is most likely circa 1300-1500. It can be dated by the places
that it designates. This one shows the Northwest corner of the US, Reykjavik
- a Viking port in Iceland, and Amelia Island. The Northwest corner of the
US has survey markers from before and after this period. If you will
remember, the Northwest corner of the US was known as early as 3100 BC
as indicated by Stonehenge and Inspiration Peak. Stonehenge, built circa
3100 BC, pointed to Inspiration Peak, Inspiration Peak revealed the
Kensington Runestone and the Kensington Runestone documented that
Inspiration Peak was 1362 miles from the Northwest corner of the US, the
Southern tip of Texas, and the Northeast corner of the US. Iceland and
Greenland were Viking ports and staging areas and Amelia Island is the
point where the 140 degree radial from Inspiration peak and the East coast
meet. This point was important in determining the Southwest corner of the
claim to the land that eventually became the US. If a line is drawn from
Bermuda through Amelia Island it will point directly to the southern tip of
Baja, California, a critical marker, along with the Southern tip of Texas,
defining the southern boundaries of what would become the United States.
The five pointed star is a sign that the creators of the geoglyph were
Christian.

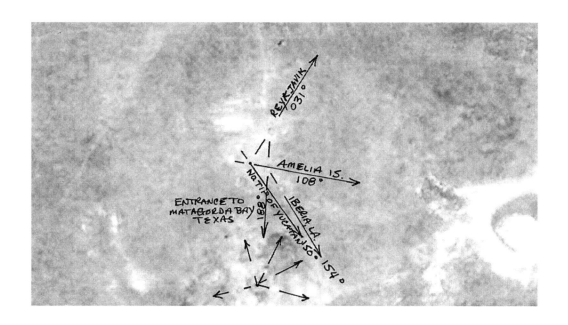

Another Weber Falls Oklahoma Geoglyph

This collection of photos show geoglyphs that are part of an extensive network of geoglyphs found around the world and within the US. The Mississippian geoglyphs, with few exceptions, outline the boundaries of the US depicting a land claim that had been planned as long ago as 3100 BC. These inland mound markers point to markers on the coast and the coastal glyphs point to other markers. These markers, both within and outside the US boundaries, form a network of geoglyphs which denote an ancient plan to one day make ,what is now the USA, a country. This fact alone should make Americans proud to be part of a plan that was formed thousands of years ago and was fought for by our forefathers to make it come true.

Further study will determine if the Mississippians were actually Vikings, Christians and Hebrew living among the early Egyptians. Curiously the Mississippian cultures begin to flourish circa 1000 AD, (The time that the Vikings departed Europe) and terminated circa 1500 AD. (The time that Europeans begin visiting America.)

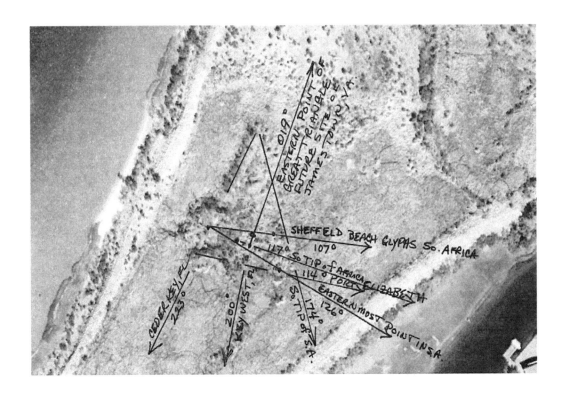

Topsail island Glyph, North Carolina

The Topsail Island geoglyph was located from the 130 degree bearing of the Baum Mound geoglyph in the next Plate. The Topsail glyph is presented to illustrate how complicated some glyphs can be. This particular one is a triangle with a large circle in the lower left corner and two smaller circles in the lower right hand corner. Between the three circles is another glyph with a mound in the center with four mounds around it. The large circle is also segmented and more radials could be taken from it if it were a little more defined. Also notice that there is another glyph, three dots (Earth mounds), forming a triangle in the upper right corner.

144

OTHER, REPRESENTATIVE, MISSISSIPPIAN MOUNDS

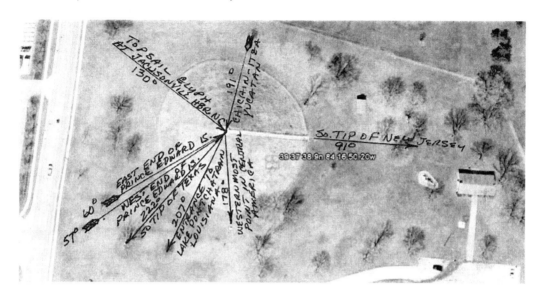

Baum Mounds, OH Geoglyph 1

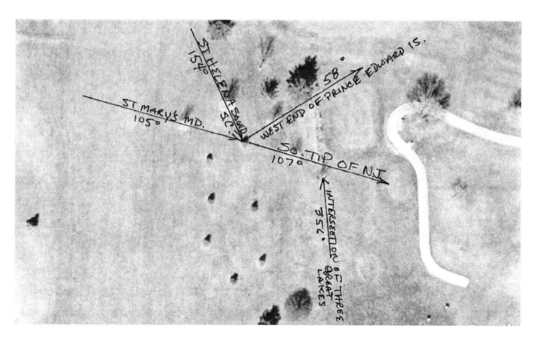

Baum Mounds, OH Geoglyph 2

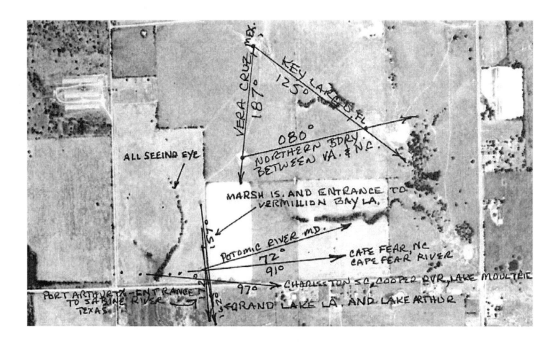

Story Point Glyph, OK

END CHAPTER

Chapter 9

The Juan de la Cosa Map

Christopher Columbus (1436-1506).

On August 3, 1492, Christopher Columbus set sail from Spain with 3 ships: the Niña, the Pinta and the Santa Maria. He used the maps and charts of a dead pilot named Alonso Sanchez and arrived on the island of Santo Domingo on Oct.12. The first to land was Martin Alonso Pinzón, the captain of the Pinta, followed by his brother Vicente Yañez Pinzón, the captain of the Niña.

On Oct. 28, he proceeded to another island named Cuba. During their stay in Cuba one of the Pinzon brothers, and his ship, disappeared for a number weeks and was not seen again until he joined Columbus and his brother as they were departing for home.

His ship was laden with gold which was given to the Pope on their return. It is believed that the missing brother went to what is now Vera Cruz to gather gold from the natives. The question arises as to how the Pinzons knew about the gold if this was their first time in the Americas.

Columbus and the Pinzons left Cuba on Jan. 2, and arrived back in Spain on March 15, 1493. Columbus never saw or set foot on the mainland of the New World until his 3rd voyage, 6 years later on August 5, 1498.

Abuse of power

Immediately after Columbus' "discovery" of the Caribbean Islands in 1492, his sponsors Ferdinand and Isabella of Spain, petitioned the Pope to give them not only the islands which Columbus had "discovered" but North and South America also, even though he supposedly had never seen either

The Catholic Church, which now held domain over most of Europe, was only too happy to comply. (The inhabitants of the New World at the time of Columbus were a Celtic alliance made up of Scotland, Cornwall, Denmark, Norway, Holland, Galicia, and Portugal.)

It just so happened that the Pope at the time, Rodrigo Borgia, was also from Spain. He drew a line from the North Pole to the South Pole, West of Africa, and gave everything West of that line to Spain. This, and the fact that Columbus sailed directly to the Southeast corner of the North American land claim, would seem to indicate that the church, through Spain, was intent on claiming North and South America for itself to the exclusion of the early colonists. This was borne out later by the fact that a representative of the church was a member of the crew of every future exploration by Spain to the Americas.

Pope Alexander VI (Rodrigo Borgia) used a document called "The Donation of Constantine" as his authority for giving the New World to Spain. No one had ever heard of this document before this time. The Catholic Pope used the political power of his office to enforce the document.

The document read in part:
"Furthermore, under penalty of excommunication late sententie to be incurred ipso facto, should anyone thus contravene, we strictly forbid all persons of whatsoever rank, even imperial and royal, or of whatsoever estate, degree, order, or condition, to dare, without your special permit or that of your aforesaid heirs and successors, to go for the purpose of trade or any other reason to the islands or mainlands, found and to be found, discovered and to be discovered, towards the west and south, by drawing and establishing a line from the Arctic pole to the Antarctic pole.... Let no one, therefore, infringe, or with rash boldness contravene, this our recommendation, exhortation, requisition, gift, grant, assignment, constitution, deputation, decree, mandate, prohibition, and will. Should anyone presume to attempt this, be it known to him that he will incur the wrath of Almighty God and of the blessed apostles Peter and Paul.

Given at Rome, at St. Peter's, in the year of the incarnation of our Lord one thousand four hundred and ninety-three, the fourth of May, and the first year of our pontificate". And so it was that Pope Alexander VI (1492-1503), the infamous Borgia, gave the New World to Spain.

On the second voyage to the New World in 1493 Christopher Columbus named as his cartographer Juan de la Cosa, who had proven his map making abilities during their first voyage.

The Explorer John Cabot

Shortly after this time the King and Queen of Spain received word that the English were about to send John Cabot on another expedition to the New World. The King and Queen had many spies in Bristol and London notifying them of the Cabot voyages and explorations in the New World.

It is presumed that the real motivation for sending Columbus to the New World was that the church found out about the information which John Cabot brought back from the New World on his previous voyages. This was confirmed by the church's actions soon after.

"The fleet he (John Cabot) prepared, which consisted of five (ships), was provisioned for a year. News came to Spain that one of these (ships), in which sailed another (Catholic) Friar Buil, has made land in Ireland in a great storm with the ship badly damaged. The Genoese kept on his way. Having seen the course they are steering and the length of the voyage, I find that what (land) they have discovered, or are in search of, is possessed by Your Highness because it is at the cape which fell to Your Highness by the convention with Portugal. It is hoped they will be back by September. I will let Your Highnesses know about it" (Pedro de Ayala letter from London).

It would appear, from the Pedro de Ayala communication, that by this time Portugal, the country that had been visiting the new world for hundreds of years with the Celts, was now aligned with Spain. This, and the Cabot explorations, would explain the timing of the first voyage of Columbus.

Ferdinand (1452-1516), King of Aragon and Isabella (1451-1504), Queen of Castile and Leon.

Ferdinand and Isabella together made up the United Kingdom of Spain. They were determined to stop the colonization of the New World, by anyone but Catholics, at any cost. Their daughter, Catherine of Aragon, eventually became the wife of Henry VIII. This marriage alliance would give them an excuse to maintain a large diplomatic mission as their eyes and ears at the London Court. Having heard of the plans of the King of England to send the explorer John Cabot out on a new expedition, Ferdinand and Isabella sent a notorious, cold blooded conquistador named Alonso de Hojeda (1468-1515) to intercept them.

Decree: "... that you go and follow that coast which you have discovered, which runs east and west, as it appears, because it goes toward the region where it has been learned that the English were making discoveries; and that you go setting up marks with the arms of their Majesties, or other signs that may be known, such as shall seem good to you, in order that it be known that you have discovered that land, so that you may stop the exploration of the English in that direction".

Hojeda set sail from Spain on May 20, 1499, with 4 ships. He was accompanied by Columbus' mapmaker Juan de la Cosa. Amerigo Vespucci also claimed to have sailed with them. They intercepted the Cabot expedition somewhere off the coast of Venezuela. All the men were killed and their maps stolen. This was a flagrant act of war by the Pope and Spain upon a peaceful voyage of discovery. Juan de la Cosa no doubt inherited all of Cabot's Maps.

Here is a quote from a Spanish historian named Martín Fernández de Navarrete:

"It is certain that Hojeda in his first voyage (that of 1499) encountered certain Englishmen in the vicinity of Coquibaçoa" (*Coleccion de los viages y descubriementos, vol. III, Madrid* 1829, p. 41). The Spanish text reads: "Lo cierto es que Hojeda en su primer viage halló á aciertos ingleses par las immediaciones de Coquibacoa" (Martin Fernandez de Navarrete).

Juan de la Cosa 1450-1610

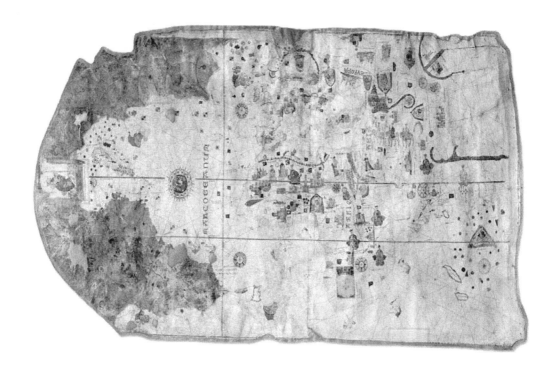

Original Colored Juan de la Cosa Map

Depicted is a photograph of the original color map.
A more defined black and white photo follows.

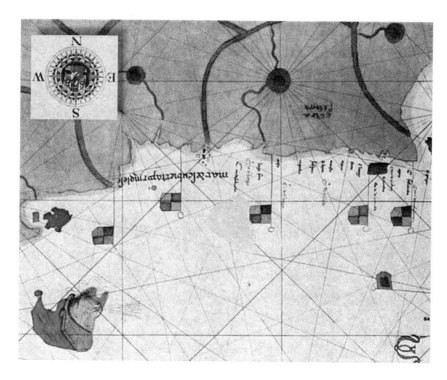

The Gulf Coast, USA, a Segment of the Juan de la Cosa Map

The first map that records Cabot's discoveries is that of Juan de la Cosa published in 1500. It is thought to be a compilation of his voyages in 1497 and 1498, from which he presumably did not return. The coastline runs east to west, with English flags marking certain named places. *"The History and the Mystery of John Cabot and the Cabot Rock"* - http://www.beyondbaccalieu.com/webpages/cabot.html

The Juan de la Cosa Map

Up to this time only the Celtic North Sea Alliance and John Cabot had charted the New World coastline. The Juan de la Cosa Map, as will be shown, is a reproduction of maps stolen from John Cabot on his last voyage to the New World. This is the oldest map of the New World, showing English flags all the way from Newfoundland to Florida. For 3 centuries it lay in the secret archives of the Vatican until it was carried to Paris by Napoleon Bonaparte in 1810.

The original parchment of this map or chart, a piece of ox-hide measuring 37.5 x 72 inches (96 X 183 cm), superbly illustrated in ink and water colors, was found in 1832 in a shop in Paris by Baron Walckenaer, a bibliophile and the Dutch Ambassador, and was brought to the attention of the world the following year by Alexander Humboldt, the famous German scholar. Upon the death of Baron Walckenaer in 1853 the map was purchased by the Queen of Spain, and though greatly deteriorated, is now the chief treasure of the Museo Naval in Madrid.

When Napoleon invaded Rome in 1810, a portion of the vast secret archives of the Vatican were taken to Paris for a world library that Napoleon planned to build. After his defeat, many of the documents were taken back to Rome but fortunately many were left behind. This map was one of the priceless items left behind and ended up in a Paris bookshop. (Ambrosini, *The Secret Archives of the Vatican* p. 291).

It is supposed that when Napoleon made his expedition to Egypt, in 1798, he also removed the contents of the ancient library at Alexandria to add to his library. This would have been the most important library, containing ancient documents, in the history of the world. However, the English hero Admiral Horatio Nelson caught Napoleon's ships by surprise in Alexandria harbor and sunk Napoleon's Flagship causing a massive explosion. It is believed that some of the most revealing ancient documents ever written were destroyed in this explosion.

The cartographic virtuoso Juan de la Cosa left us a map of the known world in 1500 that is preserved and exhibited at the Naval Museum of Madrid. It is the only known map made by a crew member of the first and second voyages of Columbus that includes a rendering of Cuba, Hispaniola, Jamaica and Puerto Rico as perceived by the instruments and knowledge of their time. The observations made by Juan de la Cosa in this region between October 12, 1492 and March 10, 1496, are recorded on this testimonial projection.

Geomagnetism and the Cartography of Juan de la Cosa:
A New Perspective on the Greater Antilles in the Age of Discovery
by Aldo Alvarez

What Juan did not realize, as he was reproducing the stolen maps of the Cabot expedition, was that he was revealing to the world the secret information that the Celts had accumulated over centuries of exploration in the Americas. This information was not recognized, until recently, due to the advent of the computer and the development of the new science of Geoglyphology.

If you will notice, on the map above, there are many small circles with a dot in the center that are depicted next to rivers all over North and South America. These dots represent geoglyphs that were placed there as land claims by the Europeans that preceded Juan to the Americas. As you can see each geoglyph is surrounded by a double lined boundary depicting a land claim which each glyph represents. In order to verify this, a search was made on each river represented on the map to see if the geoglyphs could be located. We believe that we were successful in locating each glyph in exactly the positions and on the rivers depicted on the map. As you will notice, in the photos, many glyphs have been permanently preserved, in concrete, by the cities in which they reside. Although the overall theme of the geoglyphs was not known until now, research has shown that, for the most part, government leaders have been aware of the individual glyphs in their jurisdictions for centuries. Even discounting the geoglyphs, one would have to ask the question; How could Juan depict North and South America and their rivers, a place where neither he nor Columbus visited, in such detail, in 1500. Listed below is a listing of all the geoglyph locations depicted on Juan's map. Photos of the river geoglyphs can be found in Appendix A.

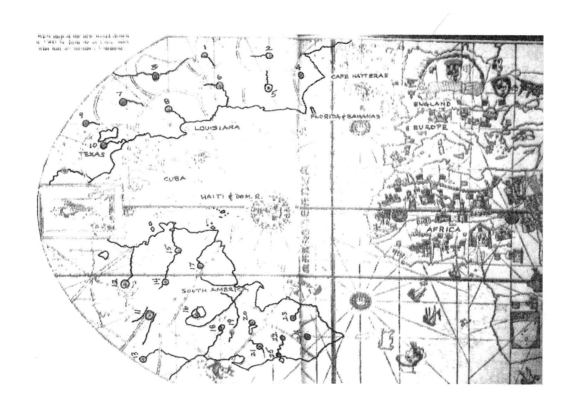

Black & White Map with River Geoglyphs Numbered

Listing of river geoglyphs with river name and coordinates stated. (See Appendix for photos.)

01. Seneca River, Phoenix, NY USA - 43 11 47.29N 76 16 52.03W
02. Delaware River, Port Jarvis, NY USA, All Seeing Eye - 41 21 23.62N 74 41 14.61W
03. Tonawanda River, Lockport, NY USA - 43 05 17.98N 78 33 46.02W
04. Urbanized Geoglyphs, Raleigh, NC USA - 35 45 40.68N 78 34 43.26W
05. Urbanized Geoglyphs, Atlanta, GA USA - 33 40 17.05N 84 39 31.12W
06. Apalachicola River, Wewahitchka, FL USA - 30 06 23.90N 85 12 51.04W
07. Ohio River, Cairo, IL USA - 36 58 58.00N 89 09 47.70W
08. Mississippi River, Alcorn MS USA - 31 51 55.55N 91 13 26.32W
09. Red River, Yarnaby, OK USA - 33 47 48.22N 96 11 22.59W
10. Sabine River, South Toledo Bend, TX USA - 31 07 21.60N 93 34 06.77W

11. The Great Circle Glyph (22 miles across), Montero, Bolivia - 17 06 57.22S 63 49 52.95W

12. Magdelena River, Barranca Bermeja, Colombia - 07 04 32.47N 73 53 11.91

13. Majes River, Pampacolca Peru - 15 42 52S 72 34 24.54W

14. Oronoco River, Cambalache, Brazil, - 08 19 50.14N 62 43 28.06W

15. Tigre River, Tucupita, Venezuela - 09 02 56.22N 62 02 56.87W

16. Pilotas River, Brazil (Through the Uruguay River) , Marcelino Ramos, Brazil - 27 28 05.48S 51 54 52.77W

17. Amazon River at the Xangu River, Brazil - 02 32 21.95S 52 04 03.42W - 03 14 44.95S 51 40 05.97W

18. Copiapo River, Copiapo, Chile - 27 27 07.23S 70 15 57.05W

19. Parana River, Rosario, Argentina - 33 16 39.62S 60 20 44.21W

20. Elqui River, Lake Puclaro, and Ruins, Vicuna Chile - 30 00 13.24S 70 49 11.18W

21. Elqui River Entrance, La Serena, Chile - 29 52 36.16S 71 16 10.19W

22. Bio-Bio River, Lija Falls, Chile 37 12 22. 81S 72 24 25.46W

23. Chubut River, Gaiman, Argentina - 43 18 06.48S 65 27 00.88W

24. Punta Arenas, Chile - 53 06 43.71S 70 53 30.50W

25. Bio-Bio River, Haulpen, Chile - 36 46 10.76S 73 02 13.26W

Photos of each geoglyph appears in Appendix A.

END OF CHAPTER

Chapter 10

The Newport Tower
and
The Kensington Runestone

Newport Tower

North America's Ancient Destiny

The solution of the Newport Tower and Kensington Runestone Mystery is much more than the solving of an ancient puzzle. It is the first step in bringing back the dignity and purpose of the great country we call the United States of America. For thousands of years the Americas have been visited, colonized, and supplied raw materials to countries in far away places. By some unknown catastrophe, most sea travel to the Americas was interrupted for an extended period of time. Sea travel to the Americas was apparently reborn in earnest again around 2nd Century BC. This was a time in which the Egyptian empire was crumbling and famine became so bad that people turned to cannibalism. This caused an exodus from Egypt which is exemplified by the many pyramids scattered around North and South America. Ernest Hemingway once remarked that; "The Egyptians have been coming to the Americas for thousands of years but were smart enough to keep it to themselves." This fact has been known by many groups throughout time but kept secret for political, philosophical and monetary reasons.

An ancient civilization, the remains of which are just now being unearthed in South America, lived in the Americas long before their European cousins returned, many millennia later. It is no accident that, after recovery from the apocalypse, Democracy, Philosophy, and Geometry were first made known by the Greeks. The Ancient Greeks were the beneficiaries and protectors of the maritime geometry and democratic philosophy passed down through the millennia. They were most likely the descendents of a group that was known as the Sea People, for lack of a true identity, that ravaged the Eastern Mediterranean circa 1200 BC. It is unknown to this day where the Sea People originated.

This is not a novel concept. Manly P. Hall authored a book on this subject titled *"The Secret Destiny of America"*, published by Penguin Group Publishers, 1944. This book is a must read for patriotic free thinkers. Manly Hall traces the origins of democracy, world travel by the ancients and the designation of North America as a special place in the destiny of the world community. The reason I mention this book is because it confirms what our research has already concluded.

In his book Hall states that man is inherently greedy and will, without self reflection and study, opt for the material things in life. Since this trait is practiced by the majority, the only way men of character can achieve the noble goal of freedom, equality and democracy is through keeping their actions secret. That's not to say all secret organizations are good, it simply means that many of the secret organizations down through time were forced into secrecy in order to prevent their noble goals from being watered down.

The Newport Tower is one such secret. The structure was constructed to preserve the noble goals of our forefathers in hope that someday the world would again come to know their plan. The solving of the Newport Tower Mystery is simply a glimmer of hope that our great nation will know, once more, the great sacrifices that have gone before to preserve democracy. It is hoped that the noble goals of our country's founders can once again be reinstated by our citizens. The decoding of the Newport Tower, and its cousin the Kensington Runestone, could not come at a better time. History tells us that all great nations eventually fall due to greed and over expansion. It is time that we, as citizens of the greatest country on earth, reaffirm our commitment to democracy and equality in order to bring peace through a commonality of purpose worldwide. Our countries noble goals are exemplified in our actions to return all land to the peoples of any country which we have liberated.

There is speculation that there will be a great change on December 21, 2012. Recent events are beginning to show a change in the way we perceive our role as masters of the Earth. Let's hope that the year 2013 will see a return to a government by the people and a degree of restraint in our unbridled consumption of the earth's resources. Our countries leaders are the only persons capable of putting this country back on a path to righteousness. Let us hope they are strong enough to prevail.

The Newport Tower

The Newport Tower has been the subject of discussion and controversy since the Colonists first arrived in the new world and discovered the structure on Rhode Island, USA. Early explorers noted that the tower existed during their early explorations of North America. However, that did not deter skeptics from claiming that the tower was constructed in Colonial times. Documented research shows that the tower was most likely constructed in the 15th Century, destroyed in the 16th Century and then rebuilt in the 17th Century on the 200th anniversary of its original construction. The Newport Tower is an important North American Landmark; however, it is the Newport Island itself that has been an important focal point of civilizations around the world for thousands of years.

Geoglyphology

The information gathered for presentation in this book was gathered using the new science of Geoglyphology. (Google keyword: Geoglyphology). The calculations performed in solving both the Newport Tower and Kensington Runestone Mystery require the use of a special software called "Google Earth". Google's software is able to calculate true spherical bearings on a curved surface and then display them correctly on a flat plane. This software can be obtained free of charge by searching the internet using the keywords "Google Earth".

Spherical Geometry

In spherical geometry all lines are curved along the surface and no lines are parallel. It is difficult to grasp the concept that two parallel headings can cross. That is because we are used to thinking in terms of Plane Geometry on a flat plane. However, this changes when you draw lines on a sphere. In dealing with a sphere you enter the realm of Spherical Geometry.

Spherical Geometry is the study of figures on the surface of a sphere, as opposed to the type of geometry studied in plane geometry or solid geometry. In spherical geometry, straight lines are great circles, so any two lines will meet in two places. There are also no parallel lines. The angle between two lines in spherical geometry is the angle between the planes of the corresponding great circles, and a spherical triangle is defined by its three angles. There is no concept of similar triangles in plane geometry.

In the field of Geoglyphology, we are plotting lines in a spherical world and then displaying the results on a flat plane. It is difficult to grasp the concept of combining Spherical Geometry with Plane Geometry. That is why the field of Geoglyphology could not have been proposed without the advent of software that computes using Spherical Geometry and then displays it on a flat plane. This type of precise mapping precludes the plotting of these bearings on a flat map. Maps become distorted when converted from a sphere to a flat map. Any lines that are depicted on a flat non-satellite map, on this website, were first plotted using the Google software and then drawn on the flat map after the end points were determined. Even then, the proper curvature is missing.

Carbon Dating

The Newport Tower has been carbon dated as being over 500 years old. The mathematics associated with the Tower, as referred to below, were found to point to four places. One is a place in Western Minnesota named Inspiration Peak, the other is an island in the Saint Lawrence Seaway, the third is Cat Island in the Bahamas, and the fourth is a point where the Equator crosses the West coast of South America. As you will see, Inspiration Peak was identified not only by the Newport Tower but also by the 5100 year old monolith Stonehenge, located in England. The stone tower itself is most likely less than 1000 years old. However, it was built as a cornerstone to mark a land claim that was conceived thousands of years ago.

*Results of Carbon Dating on the Newport Tower are located in **Appendix B***

Newport Tower was built by early inhabitants of North America for two reasons. The first was to point the way to Inspiration Peak, a place of special geographical importance. The second was to substantiate the builders land claim to North America by using the unique geographical location of Newport, RI USA. The predecessors of the people that built the tower knew of the North American Territorial Claim, as well as the rest of the world, for over 10,000 years. This is substantiated by 10th century ruins in South America and Africa that tie into Inspiration Peak, as well as the Newport Tower site. For some reason North America held some special significance. Geoglyphs found around the world show that people were mapping out what would later be known as the United States at least as far back as the building of the Stonehenge monolith in the United Kingdom. Monoliths located in Central America outline the boundaries of what would eventually become the boundaries of the United States.

Ancient geoglyphs found in Mesoamerica, Baja California, and Central America outlines the original boundaries of a North American Colony. Circa 1559 the original boundaries of the North American Territory would change. The reason for the change of boundaries was apparently the result of the attack on Mexico City by Hernando Cortez and Spain in 1519. The inhabitants of the Colonies were not able to respond because they had not yet developed their military force to the point where they could retaliate.

That would come later, at the cost of loosing Baja California and Central America while reclaiming the Western US from Spain and the Central US from France and England.

A 7000 year old glyph located in Western Africa pointed out the location where the Newport Tower would eventually be built 6500 years later. (See below) Gavin Menzies book *"1421, The Year China Discovered America"* adds credence to the argument that Europeans or Egyptians, and their descendents, inhabited the Americas long before history is willing to admit. Menzies quotes from the year 1524 logs of the Italian explorer Verrazano. The following passage refers to Verrazano's stay in what later became Newport, Rhode Island:

"The local people were the color of brass, some of them inclined more to whiteness... . The women are of like conformity and beauty; very handsome and well favored, of pleasant countenance and comely to behold; they are well-mannered and content as any woman, and of good education... . The women used other kinds of dressing themselves like unto the women of Egypt and Syria; ... ."

Menzies goes on to say: ...*"Verrazano was not describing local women married to foreigners, but women resembling those from the East who had somehow ended up in North America. Clearly they were from a different civilization and were not natives of North America".*

The book infers that these women were left there by the Chinese 100 years before. However, the women that the Chinese were carrying were concubines used to make money when the Chinese were in port. That would hardly fit the character, or the dress, of the Rhode Island women. It would however fit the character and dress of the Europeans and their Egyptian cousins.

An Ancient Egyptian Geoglyph That Identified the Future Newport Tower Site 7000 years before the tower was built.

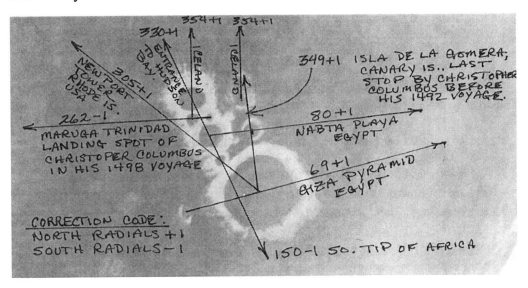

The 7000 Year Old Gulfo de Cintra Glyphs, Western Sahara, Africa
(23 01 32.58 N - 16 07 04.69 W)

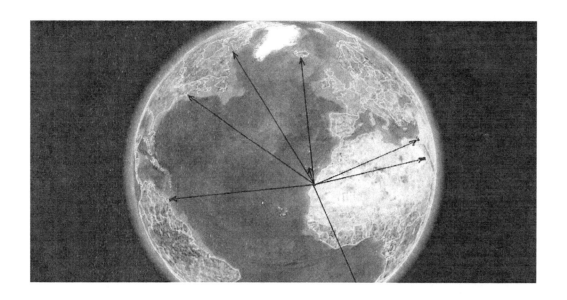

The Gulfo de Cintra Glyph, Radial End Points

The Gulfo de Cintra geoglyphs are some of the most spectacular that we have encountered in all our investigations around the world. First of all they are very clear. There is no doubt where the centers of the defining circles are. This is due to the fact that there is very little erosion in the area. Secondly, all the resulting radials point to well established markers that leave no doubt as to where they were intended to point. The Gulfo de Cintra Glyph was discovered by following the directions from a 7000 year old Egyptian Monolith that has been identified and accurately dated by accredited archeologists.

As stated in the Stonehenge article below the most important glyphs require a uniform correction of a few degrees on all the bearings. This is to preclude the uninformed from reading the glyph. In the Gulfo de Cintra Glyph the code is to add one degree to all bearings from 271 to 090, and subtract one degree from all bearings from 091 to 270. It is obvious that ancient civilizations were able to understand things that we are just beginning to understand. If you will remember, in your history studies, the Hebrews were involved in the engineering and oversight of the building of the pyramids. Did the Egyptians, Hebrews, Greeks, Celts, and early Christians have some knowledge that others did not have? The geoglyphs located around the world indicate that the answer is yes.

THE GEOMETRY OF THE NEWPORT TOWER

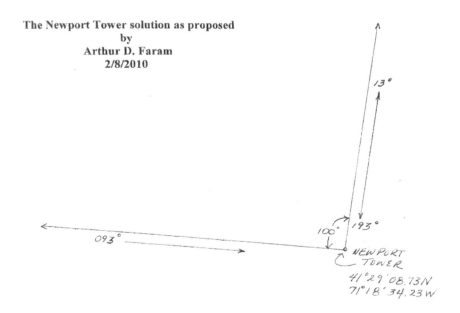

The Newport Tower solution as proposed
by
Arthur D. Faram
2/8/2010

The Newport 013 Radial

Something that must be remembered about the builders of the tower is that they place little or no value on words. The builders, their predecessors and descendents, are men of numbers and symbols. You should also know that the builders, and their predecessors, never present a puzzle without setting up another solution to the same puzzle by some other method. This prevents the skepticism that has prevailed over the past centuries about the Newport Tower and other ancient artifacts which no verification from another source has been found, until now. It is a known fact that the Newport Tower is aligned along a 93/273 degree axis. In addition there has always been a question as to why most European structures, of non-secular origin, have six legs while this one has eight legs. Remembering a bit of information from my research in Europe I decided to apply that information to the Newport Tower to see if it applied. The saying went like this; "The treasure lies under a giant triangle that is so large that only God can see it". This seemed like a good place to start looking for a triangle. I personally have always thought that the treasure would be something more meaningful than a monetary treasure. It seems I was right. As you will see later that treasure is the USA, which lies under, what I call, "The Great Triangle". (See below)

My assumption was that the eight legs on the tower were a symbol for 80 degrees. Navigators of this era oriented their maps and alignments to the East. As a result the solution was started by subtracting 80 degrees from the East bearing of 93 degrees. This obviously left a bearing of 13 degrees. If this was correct there now existed one angle, and two sides of undefined length, to a triangle. In order for the 13 degree radial to be significant a geographical location along the 13 degree bearing would have to be found to define the length of that side of the triangle. The 273 degree radial was not considered, figuring that someone would have already figured that one out.

An explanation of Magnetic Deviation and why True Headings are used in Geoglyphology is located in **Appendix C**.

La Haute-Cote-Nord
(48 23 53.32N 68 52 04.17W)

While tracing along the 13 degree bearing it was noticed that the line went directly over a small island in the Saint Lawrence Seaway named "La Haute-Cote-Nord". La Haute-Cote -Nord, loosely translated, means "The Highest Point on the North Dimension". This appeared to be a vital clue. If so there now existed two sides, one length and one angle of the triangle. But in order to make a triangle one more angle or length was needed. While studying the area around the island it was discovered that there were five more locations in the Saint Lawrence Seaway named La Haute-Cote-Nord. It was evident that three of the locations formed the vertexes of a triangle. The three geographical points were connected to see what developed. The result can be seen in the next frame.

The La Haute Triangle

The resulting triangle consisted of three interior angles of 20, 60 and 100 degrees. Since 100 degrees was the one angle that had already been decoded from the Newport Tower it was decided to apply the other two angles to the partially completed triangle to see what developed. The East/West leg of the triangle was extended to the West because to the East there was nothing but water. If a significant landmark existed at the point of the Western vertex a solution to the mystery of the Newport Tower may have been found. The resulting triangle is in the next frame.

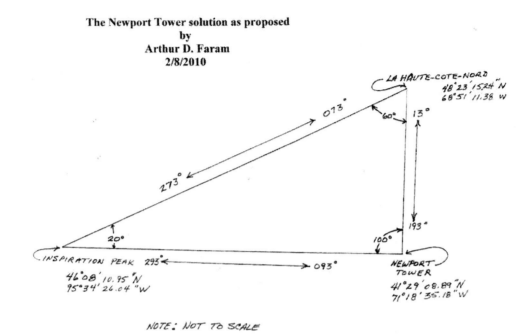

The Newport Tower solution as proposed
by
Arthur D. Faram
2/8/2010

LA HAUTE-COTE-NORD
48° 23' 15.24" N
68° 51' 11.38" W

INSPIRATION PEAK
46° 08' 10.95" N
95° 34' 26.04" W

NEWPORT TOWER
41° 29' 08.89" N
71° 18' 35.18" W

NOTE: NOT TO SCALE

The Newport Triangle

As hoped, there was a significant landmark situated right under the Western vertex of the triangle. The name of that landmark is Inspiration Peak. A diagram of the Newport Triangle appears above. Two other triangles supporting the Newport Triangle solution are shown below. They were located in areas known to have been colonized by early European settlers.

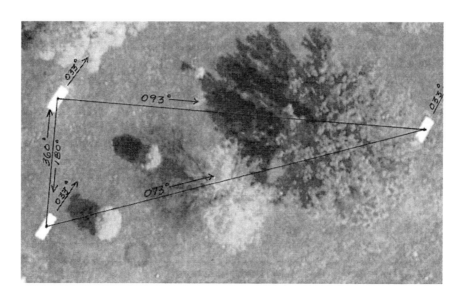

The Cemetery Triangle

This triangle is made up of three 15th century European graves. The graves are located in the state of Maryland, the second "recorded colony" to be settled in what would become the United States. This triangle identifies itself as an important clue by the fact that all three graves are oriented to 33 degrees and point to the ancient maritime port of Reykjavik, Iceland. Reykjavik was the prime port located midway between Europe and the Americas and was the stopping place for most ships, in the North Atlantic, transiting from Europe to the Americas. The important clue is that the triangle provides two of the three bearings that make up the Newport Triangle. This just one more check to substantiate that the solution to the Newport Triangle is valid.

The Capiapo Chili Triangle

This triangle is located in Capiapo, Chili. There are many glyphs scattered around the globe as clues to substantiate the Newport Triangle solution. These are but two of them.

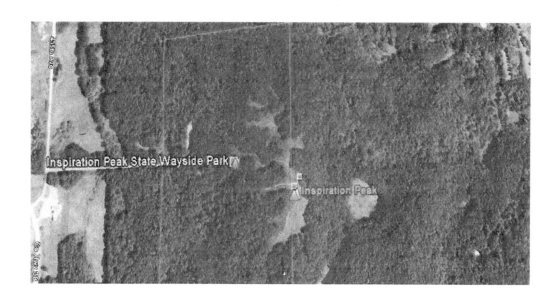

Inspiration Peak
(46 08 09.49N 95 34 14.61W)

Inspiration Peak has been visited for over 5000 years as a spiritual meeting place. The existence of Inspiration Peak in ancient times is verified by the monolith Stonehenge in England. The dating of Stonehenge has already been established as circa 3100 BC by celebrated scientists and archeologists around the world and should not present fuel for controversy. Inspiration Peak was not only identified by the complex mathematics built into the Newport Tower, but is also identified by many other glyphs around the world. This also holds true for the site where the Newport Tower resides. (See below)

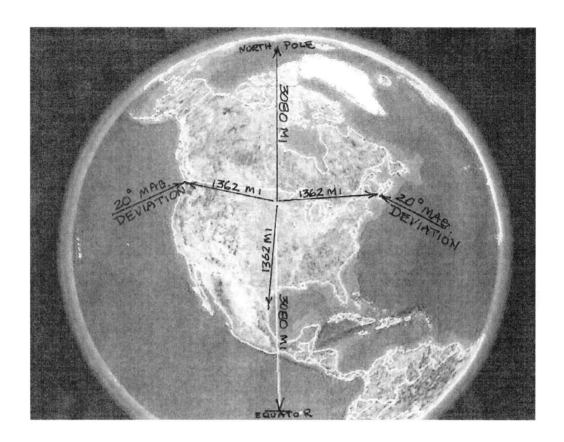

The Incredible Inspiration Peak Survey Marker
(From information imprinted on the Kensington Runestone, see Part 2)

Inspiration Peak is not only an spiritual meeting place but also serves as a survey marker for a land claim that stakes out the choicest part of North America for the people that created it. By now I'm sure you have noticed that this land claim coincides with what is now the continental United States of America. Please note that not only is the marker equidistant from the equator and the North Pole and the three corners of what is now known as the USA, but that both the Northern corners of the survey are located on lines of 20 degrees of magnetic deviation. What genius did this survey?

The importance of Inspiration Peak is further expressed by the fact that at every 10 degree increment, at a distance of 22.7 miles around the Peak, there exist markers that, if lighted at night, could have been used to identify the Peak from above. The next three photos show the marker on the 360 degree radial at 22.7 miles from Inspiration Peak.

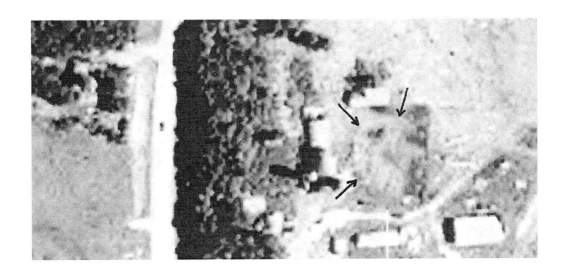

The 360 Degree Marker in 2003

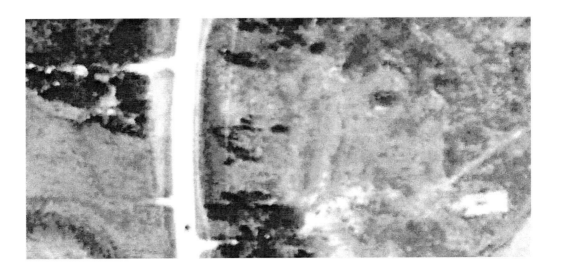

The 360 Degree Marker Today

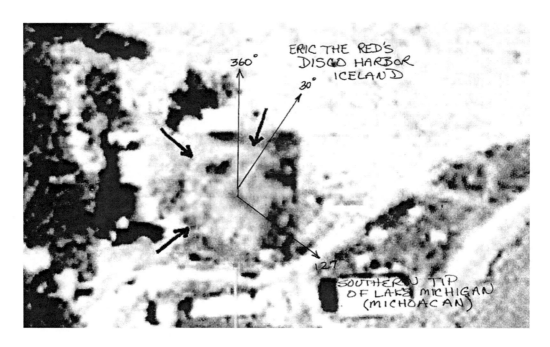

The Extended Radials of the Two Lines in the Center of the Marker

The marker on the 360 degree bearing of Inspiration Peak leaves no doubt the Vikings penetrated deep into North America during the early years of their exploration of the Americas. The marker does, however, raise another question. Was the marker already there and the Vikings simply modified it, or did the Vikings place all the markers around Inspiration Peak? Curiously, the marker points to the same spot to which Diego Rivera's Mural "Michoacan" points. I can't get it out of my head how similar the names Michoacan and Michigan are. The fact that they are connected by many geoglyphs around the world leads me to believe there is a connection.

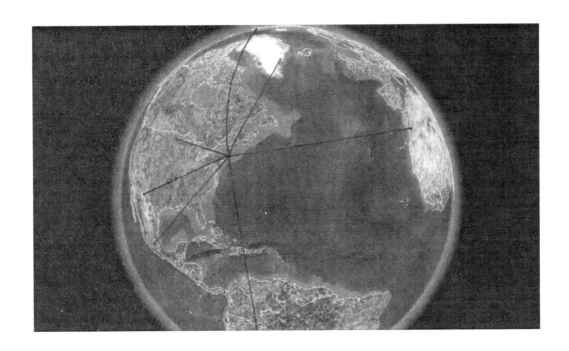

**Photo showing known origination points of geoglyphs
that point to the Newport Tower Location**

Origination points for the pointers displayed in the above photo. Included are the approximate dates the pointers were created.

Gulfo de Cintra Geoglyphs, Sahara West Africa - c7000BC
Inspiration Peak, Minnesota USA - c7000BC - 3100BC
Cahuachi, Nazca Peru - c5AD
Pyramids of China - c100BC - 400AD
Tiniteqilaq Geoglyph, Greenland - c1100AD
River Geoglyph El Paso, Texas USA - c1300
Mexico City Geoglyph - c1325AD
Kensington Runestone, Minnesota USA - c1473AD
"Michoacan", Mexico, Mural Glyph by Diego Rivera - c1925

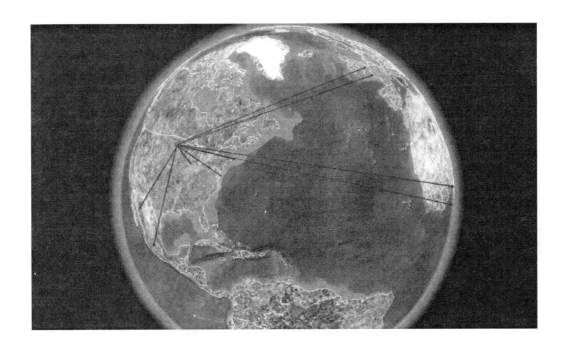

**Photo showing known origination points of geoglyphs
that point to the Inspiration Peak Location**

Origination points for the pointers displayed in the above photo. Included are
the approximate dates the pointers were created.

Stonehenge Monolith, UK - c3100BC
Monte Alban Pyramid, Oaxaca Mexico - c500BC
Pigeon Point Geoglyph, Minnesota USA - c1200AD
Manchester, Ohio Geoglyph USA - c1300AD
Kensington Runestone, Minnesota USA - c1362AD
23rd Street NW Geoglyph, Washington DC USA - c1400AD
Point du Raz Geoglyphs, Bretagne, France - c1400AD
Malabo Island Geoglyphs, Equatorial New Guinea, West Africa - c1400AD
Cape of Good Hope Geoglyphs, South Tip of Africa - c1400AD
Atanacio Geoglyphs, Mexico - c1400AD
Newport Tower, Newport, RI USA - c1473AD

STONEHENGE

Stonehenge is located in the South Central portion of England and is centrally located in the Western Celtic Geographic Arena. Stonehenge has been accurately dated by renowned scientists as being approximately 5100 years old. For Millennia visitors have speculated about the purpose of Stonehenge. Up to this point the purpose has generally been speculated to be some type of celestial calendar. There is no doubt that the monolith is a form of celestial calendar. However, new evidence suggests that it is much more than that. Stonehenge in addition to being a celestial calendar, like Inspiration Peak and The Newport Tower, is also a world class survey marker. (See the following Plates.)

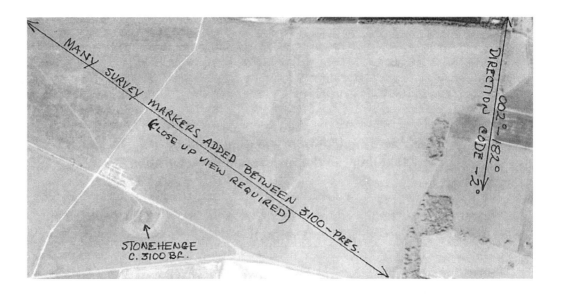

The above plate shows Stonehenge and a portion of the area North of the Monument. The entire surrounding area is covered with glyphs of various symbols and lines. All symbols point to what research has shown to be geographical landmarks significant in the history of the Nordics and their descendents. It appears that these particular markers may be part of a burial process. This is deduced from the fact that the Nordic graves in the Americas have at least one pointer pointing to a Celtic occupied place in Europe, while the pointers in the fields around Stonehenge point to locations outside Britain. Whether these indicate the place the subject was born, visited or died will require further research. Another reason for this particular plate is to show the Direction Code in the upper right hand corner of the plate. Many similar sites around the world include at least one pointer that points to, or within a few degrees of, one of the four cardinal points on the compass. This is to let the interpreter of the site know how many degrees to add or subtract from the radials at that particular glyph to make it accurate. In this case it is the hedge row, the shrubs most likely added later, which is aligned in a 002/182 degree orientation. That indicates that the interpreter must subtract 2 degrees from all the pointers at the Stonehenge site for them to point where the originator intended for them to point. It has been found that most sites contain this Direction Code, however, only the most important sites require an addition or subtraction from the cardinal direction.

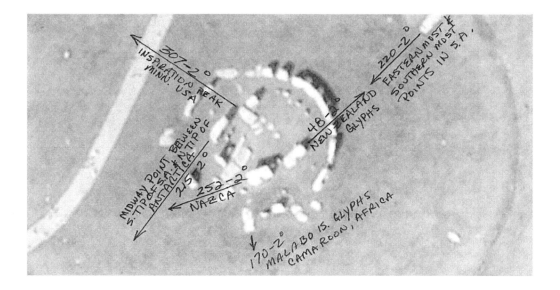

Stonehenge, UK (51* 10' 43.92"N 1* 49' 34.36"W)

This plate shows a view of Stonehenge from above with radials projected from the major stones. Although the locations indicated here may seem insignificant, they will grow in significance as you become more familiar with the glyphs. As you can see there are many more pointers that have not been drawn out. The main point of this illustration is to indicate the relationship of Stonehenge to Inspiration Peak.

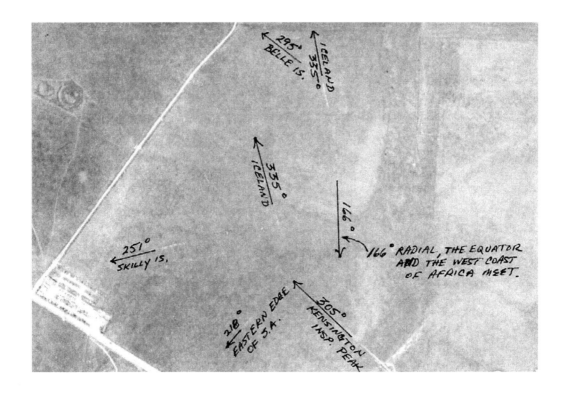

**This plate shows just a few symbols and their associated
pointers in the field North of the Stonehenge Monument.**

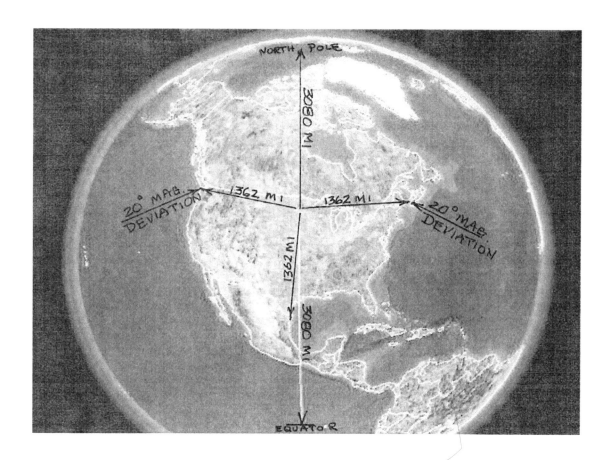

The Surveyed Location of Inspiration Peak

Inspiration Peak lies halfway between the Equator and the North Pole. In addition, the two Northern 1362 mile long radials mark the NW and NE corners of the original North American Land Claim, which would later become the boundary between the US and Canada. If this was not enough the East/West line that is the border between what would become the border between Canada and the US terminates on both ends at points that have exactly 20 degrees of magnetic deviation. For a culture to be able to locate and survey this location over 5000 years ago boggles the mind. This was one of the survey markers which verified a claim to North America as far back as 3100 BC. Around 100 AD an effort was begin in earnest to further substantiate the land claim in the Americas. This can be verified in the orientations of various glyphs in Central America constructed Circa 100 AD, as well as the information inscribed on the Kensington Runestone and the orientation of the Newport Tower, apparently constructed circa 1472. The Newport Tower and Kensington Runestone are the most important of the markers which have been found in North America. They are important because these two markers are able to combine together to delineate the North American land claim as it existed when Stonehenge built and as it existed after it was modified following the Spanish invasion of Mexico.

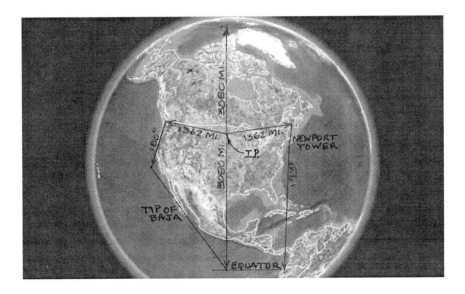

Inspiration Peak, Minnesota USA - The North American Territory Established Sometime Between 10,000 BC and 3150 BC.

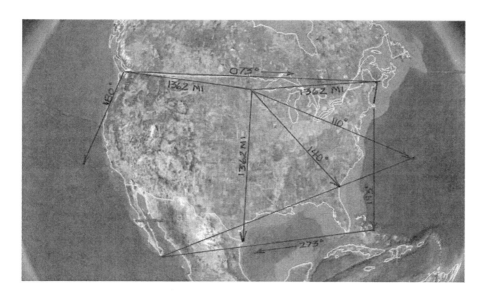

**Inspiration Peak, USA - Revised North American Territory - Circa 1559
After the Spanish Conquest of Mexico in 1515.**

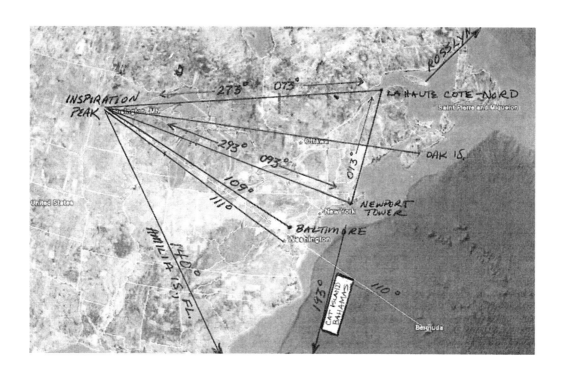

Inspiration Peak Radials as Defined after 1559.

In the previous Plate all the bearings associated with solving of the Newport Tower and the Kensington Runestone mysteries are depicted. The 013 degree bearing was the initial bearing that had to be discovered before the puzzles could be solved. The reciprocal of the 013 degree bearing is the 193 degree bearing which will become important in defining the claim to North America. In the solving of the puzzle the magnetic bearings of 073 and 273 degrees became known. (See above) They are not reciprocal headings because they originate from two different points on the earths surface and are affected by magnetic deviation. In the decoding of the Kensington Runestone, which verified the math in the Newport Tower solution, the bearings of 110 and 140 were also mentioned. Note that the 111 radial, which usually represents the Trinity, goes through the current capitol of the USA. This could not have been a coincidence.

It is from the data in the previous Plate, drawn out on a map similar to the one that follows, from which, in about 1559 the early colonizers of North America staked their final claim to what turned out to be the United States. Christopher Columbus, working for Spain and the Pope, was chosen, along with the Pizon brothers, to visit the Southeast corner of this land claim (See next Plate) and claim the land for Spain and the Church. The fact that Columbus and the Pizon Brothers visited two of the four island ports which were highlighted by the "Gulfo de Cintra" glyphs, proves that these islands were known and in use, most likely as resupply ports, prior to their explorations..

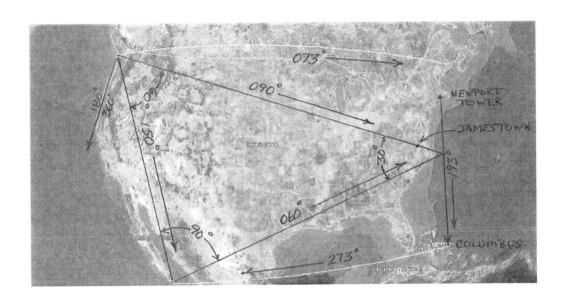

Map of the North America Land Claim and the Great Triangle

This diagram points out the land claim devised by the early inhabitants of North America circa the 16th Century. The claim is bounded on the East by the 013/193 degree radial that runs through the Newport Tower to Cat island in the Bahamas, on the South by the 273 degree radial which runs West from where the 193 degree radial intersects Cat Island in the Bahamas, and the 073 degree radial which runs from the Northwest corner of the US to the Northeast corner of the US. The Western limits are defined by the 360/180 degree radial. If you will notice, the 193, 273 and 073 degree radials are all duplicated in the Newport Triangle solution. Just another cross check devised by the early inhabitants of North America. The Southwest corner of the claim, that is the tip of Baja California, is additionally defined by running a line between the termination points of the 140 degree radial and the 110 degree radial mentioned on the Kensington Runestone. The termination point for the 110 degree radial is Bermuda. The termination point for the 140 degree radial is the point where the 140 degree bearing crosses the East Coast (Amelia Island). By running a line between the Bahamas termination point and the Amelia Island termination point the line ends precisely at the tip of Baja California. This is just another cross check which the originators included to prove to the interpreter that they were on the right track. Now, if a line is drawn between the Northwest corners of the claim to the Southwest corner of the claim a line running on a 150 degree heading is created. If a 90 degree vertex is added to the Southwest end of the line and a 60 degree vertex is added to the Northwest end of the line a perfect 30/60/90 Right Triangle is created. As if this were not enough the 30/60/90 triangle terminates on the 193 degree radial from the Newport Tower. This type of triangle is considered the perfect triangle, and an icon, by the ancients. Also, it cannot be a coincidence that the first "historically recorded" colony in the USA, Jamestown, VA lies under one leg of the triangle.

It is no coincidence that the SE corner of the land claim was where Columbus landed to claim this ancient land claim for Spain before the early colonists were strong enough to resist. Nor is it a coincidence that Jamestown, the first "historically recorded" colony in the USA, was located under a leg of the 30/60/90 degree triangle by the early colonists. It is clear that the 15th Century colonists were attempting to establish an irrefutable land claim to the land that eventually became the United States. Please note that the original claim by the ancients, much earlier than the 15th Century colonizers, extended from the Equator to the Current boundary between the USA and Canada. Succeeding events limited this claim to within the three 1362 mile long pointers and caused the loss of Central America and Baja California.

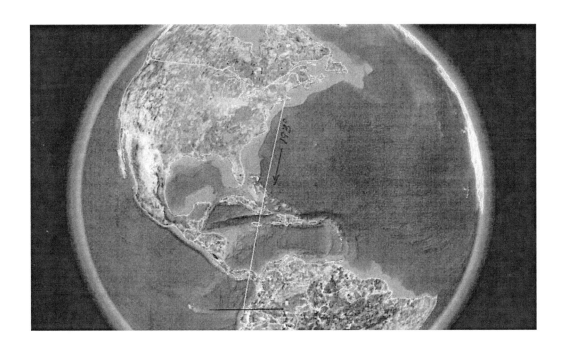

The Newport Tower 193 Degree Radial

Further confirmation that the 193 Degree Radial was not chosen at random is the fact that when extended to the South it intersects exactly at where the Equator crosses the coast of Ecuador. This point has been confirmed as an important marker to the ancients and is identified by numerous glyphs around the world.

THE EXPEDITION OF SIR FRANCIS DRAKE

In 1577 Sir Francis Drake of England was commissioned by Queen Elizabeth to make a top secret mission to the Americas. The penalty for leaking information on the voyage was death. The crew was told that they were going to the Mediterranean; however, they sailed right past Gibraltar. It was then that the crew was told that they were going to the New World. Drake sailed around South America and up the coast of Chile and Peru, raiding Spanish colonies, and ships, for gold and wine along the way. By the time Drake reached Mexico he had so much gold that his ship could hold no more.

Rather than returning to England, Drake continued up the coast of California, Oregon and Washington, stopping along the way at various inlets. Drake's voyage is documented, not by Drake, but by the Spanish who later retraced his route up the coast, stopping along the way and speaking to natives with whom Drake had contact. This is documented in *"The Principal Navigations"*, Hakluyt 1589. In the Hakluyt document it is mentioned that Drake was searching for an entrance to the mainland called the Strait of Juan de Fuca. This body of water separates the US from Vancouver, Canada and is the precise point where the Northwest corner of the North American Land Claim exists. Don't forget, this land claim was surveyed before 3100 BC and was revised c1500 AD (See Map Below)

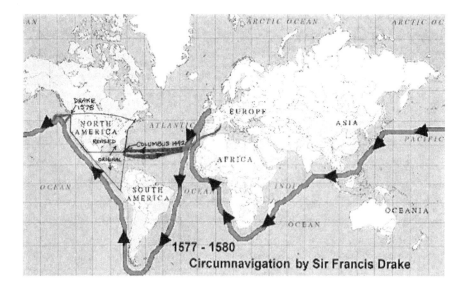

A map of the Voyages of Christopher Columbus and Sir Francis Drake.

As you may have noticed Columbus went directly to what would become the Southeast Corner of the Revised North American Territory and Drake went to the Northwest corner of the North American Territory. When you consider they had the entire world in which to navigate this goes way past the realm of coincidence. If you will remember the Celtic alliance, which originally included Portugal, had left Spain and England out of their plans to colonize the Americas. Shortly after the Voyage of Columbus, who carried the Spanish flag, Spain, now in alliance with Portugal, invaded Central and

South America. Whether by necessity, or by agreement with Portugal, the Nordic residents of North America revised their territorial boundaries North, to within a few miles of where Columbus was reported to have first landed.

By the time Drake, who carried the English flag, left on his expedition in 1577 AD, Central and South America were being colonized by Portugal and Spain. The Nordic inhabitants of the New World had revised their territorial boundaries to exclude Spanish occupied Mesoamerica. It is presumed that England now had plans to acquire the revised North American Territory and sent Drake to place their survey markers along the West coast of North America. Drake left markers along the West coast including a brass plaque somewhere in California. Now when England began colonizing the East coast of the revised North American Territory, they would have their banners on both the East and West coast. This would ostensibly give England claim to the North American Territory.

Further proof that the English had a long range plan for North America was that when Drake returned to England his entire voyage was kept secret. Here is a man that made the first recorded circumnavigation of the earth, had brought the Queen tons of gold, fought and won against the Spanish in their own backyard and now he and his crew were sworn to secrecy under penalty of death. All of Drakes logs, charts and maps were confiscated and have never been seen again.

Spain and England, at the time, were the most powerful countries in the world. The North American colonists had no choice but to accept whatever fate was thrust upon them. History is testimony to the purpose, determination and strategy of the founding fathers of the future United States that they prevailed in the face of such overwhelming odds.

RUYSCH'S 1508 MAP of NEWPORT, RHODE ISLAND USA

(As It Appeared During Cabot's Voyage in 1498 AD)

Cabot's Terra Nova (New Land)

More evidence that Newport, Rhode Island USA was the hub of North American activity in ancient times is the map of the world made in 1508 by Johannes Ruysch. This is the second oldest map still in existence showing the New World, the Juan de la Cosa map being the oldest. They were both made from data gathered by John Cabot before he disappeared on his last voyage. On Ruysch's map, he shows "Terra Nova" or "New Land". This is supposed to be the place where Cabot landed when he came to North America in 1498.

Many colonies have claimed that their city is the one where Cabot spent his time in North America, especially Newfoundland. The Faram Research Foundation has been able to locate the area from which the Ruysch map was made. As is our custom, we try to provide physical proof of any new discoveries that are made. The photo below depicts Newport, Rhode Island USA as it is today. The map is marked with nine separate points of reference that match the Ruysch Map, including the three hills marked on the Island of Newport.

It quickly becomes obvious that the two Capes, marked on the map as C. de Portogesi and C. Glaciato, are missing on the modern map of Newport. There could be three reasons for this; One reason for this occurrence is that the two Capes were man made in order to form the two geoglyphs and have since eroded away due to the earth fill being too soft to withstand the elements. The second reason could be that someone did not want the two geoglyphs, which were constructed to point back to the port from which the colonist came, to be discovered. The third reason could be that the inhabitants used the earth to backfill the inlet just North of Cape Portogesi. If you will notice, the South Cape is named for Portugal and the North Cape is named for Galicia. As has been mentioned many times in this book, Portugal and Galicia were the leaders of the Celtic North Sea Alliance. The Celtic Danes are responsible for forming the Viking Empire as their military arm and are responsible, along with the Vikings and the other members of the alliance for the colonization of the Northeastern portion of North America, long before either Columbus or Cabot.

To further emphasize this point, the circles (Capes) labeled as Portogesi and Galaciato were formed to point to the Capitol of the Portuguese and Galician alliance, Lisbon Portugal, the Western most city in Portugal. (See Below)

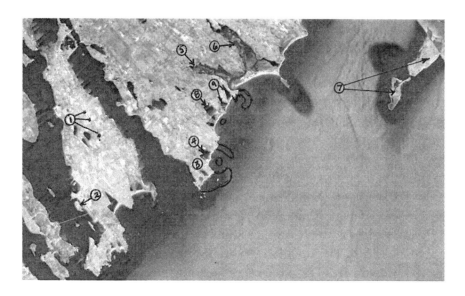

Newport, Rhode Island USA, Today
Geoglyphs, missing for the reasons stated above, are inked in.)

Portuguese Geoglyphs
(Constructed prior to 1508, claiming the new land for Portugal)

The combination of mathematics, geometry, and survey skills necessary to accomplish such a perfect geometrical puzzle is phenomenal. By including both the Kensington Runestone and Inspiration Peak in the Newport Tower Solution the originators are not only showing their skill but as usual providing a crosscheck to verify to any investigator that they have the correct solution to the land claim. As stated before the early colonizers of America always provide a way of verifying their work.

By the time you finish reading the Kensington Runestone solution (Described below) you should be convinced that the Kensington Runestone and the Newport Tower both compliment and verify the credibility of each other. It is obvious that the evidence shows a time consuming survey of North America. A prudent person would have to question who did it, when did they do it, and why. The answers are astonishing, but not surprising, and if the overwhelming evidence is accepted by historians it will change the history books forever.

The Kensington Runestone

"An Ancient Mystery Solved"

The Kensington Runestone

The Kensington Runestone was found by a Swedish farmer, named Olof Ohman, in 1898 while clearing land for his farm near Kensington, Minnesota (45* 48' 46.17"N - 95* 40' 01.53"). Due to inherent skepticism, and the fact that Olof was Swedish, many people thought the stone was a forgery. This controversy has existed for over 100 years up until this very time. Well the controversy is over. There is now physical proof that the runestone is authentic and plays a large role in American history.

The Kensington Runestone, pictured above, is 31 inches high, 16 inches wide, six inches thick and weighs 202 pounds. On the face and one side are characters known as "runes", a type of writing used in the Middle Ages only by inhabitants of northwestern Europe, such as the Norwegians, Danes, and Gotland Islanders.

If you have read about the Newport Tower you will now understand how the Kensington Runestone fits into that puzzle. As the Newport Tower was used to establish the location of one of the most important locations of the early inhabitants of North America, Inspiration Peak, so the Kensington Runestone is also used to locate, validate, and provide critical information for that same location. As has been said many times, the builders of these markers never provide only one solution to a puzzle. There is always more than one solution to a puzzle in order to validate the first.

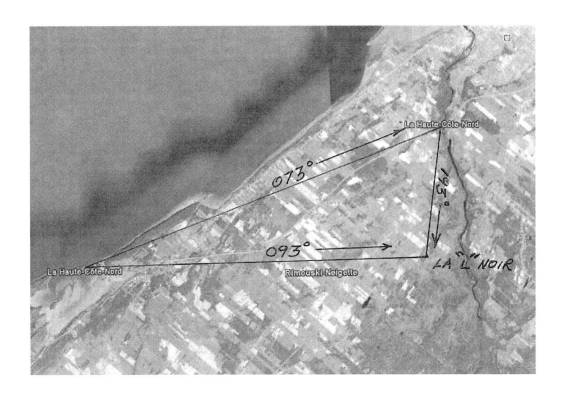

The La Haute Triangle 2

As you learned in the Newport Tower presentation the tower points out six
locations on the Saint Lawrence Seaway named "La Haute-Cote-Nord".
Four of these locations were used to solve the Newport Tower mystery. That
left two more that had to be explained. A line was drawn between the two
remaining locations. Upon examination it was found that the line was
aligned in a 073 Degree orientation. Remembering that 073 was the same
bearing as one of the legs of the Newport Triangle the same vertex angles
were applied to the 073 degree line. The bearings of the legs of the triangle
were extended in six different directions with no interesting landmarks that
would indicate that the triangle was useful. That is when it was decided to
look on the ground. (See next Plate)

La "L" Noir (The Black "L")

Surprisingly, right under the East vertex of the triangle was a marking resembling the letter "L". The bearings of the figure were extended to determine if they pointed to any significant landmarks. The results are depicted in the frame above. The one I was most interested in was the one that pointed to another island, similar to the "La Haute-Cote- Nord" island encountered while solving the Newport Tower puzzle. If you will remember the translation of "La Haute-Cote-Nord" was "The High Dimension North" and was the northernmost point on the 013 degree radial from the Newport Tower. The name of this new point was "Cote-Nord-Hauter". The translation of the name of this island is "The Higher North Dimension". Unfortunately the name tags for these locations mysteriously disappeared from Google Earths displays shortly after their publication. They can be seen in the previous Plate titled "La Haute Triangle 2".

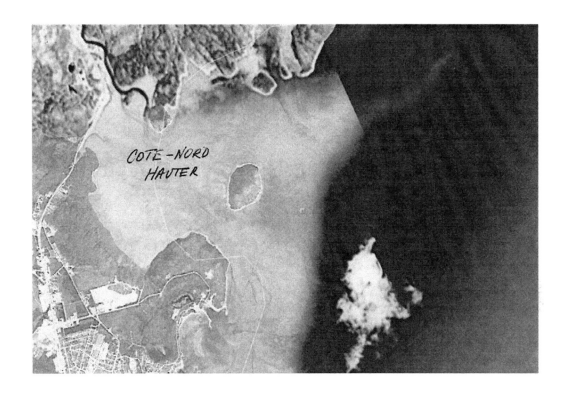

Cote-Nord Hauter
(48 45 06.12N 69 01 59.98W)

The name "Cote-Nord-Hauter" is the name of an island directly across the Saint Lawrence Seaway from La Haute-Cote-Nord, the island that defined the end point for the first side of the Newport Triangle. Could this be the end point for another radial from the Newport Tower? A line was drawn between the new island and the Newport Tower. The bearing of the new radial from the tower was 012 degrees, one degree less than the original bearing of 013 degrees. On a hunch, another triangle was drawn alongside the Newport Tower Triangle by subtracting exactly one degree from the bearing of each side to see where it would point.

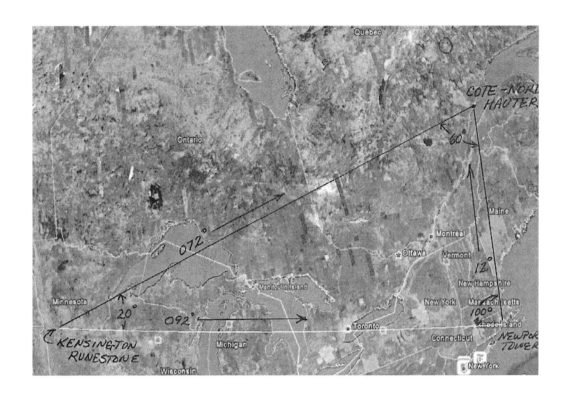

The Kensington Triangle

Sure enough, once the new triangle was drawn the place where the Kensington Runestone was found lay directly beneath the Western tip of the triangle. For this to be meaningful it would now be necessary to determine why, and how, the Kensington Runestone and the Newport Tower were connected.

Runestone Front

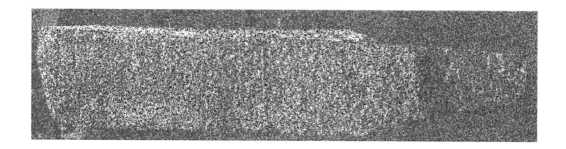

Runestone Side

199

Upon submitting the runestone to a handwriting analysis it was determined that the writing had been done by two different persons. The first five rows were done by one person and the last four rows, and side, were done by a second person. The first tip off is the slant of the work. If you will check the slant in the pictures above you will notice a distinct difference from one persons writing to the other. Another tip off is the way the letters are formed. For example the first person brings the right leg of his "R" all the way down to the baseline. The second person stops short of the baseline. As is common when someone is attempting to copy another person's writing, the first half of the sixth line is similar to the first five lines. But as is always the case, the forger gets tired of trying to copy the other person's style and towards the end of the first line and thereafter he reverts back to his own style.

Text (Nielsen interpretation)
With one slight variation from the Larsson rune rows, using the letter þ (representing "th" as in "think" or "this") instead of d, the inscription on the face (from which a few words may be missing due to spalling, particularly at the lower left corner where the surface is calcite rather than greywacke) reads:

" 8:göter:ok:22:norrmen:po:
??o:opþagelsefarþ:fro
vinlanþ:of:vest:vi:
haþe:läger:veþ:2:skylar:en:
þags:rise:norr:fro:þeno:sten:
vi:var:ok:fiske:en:þagh:äptir:
vi:kom:hem:fan:10:man:röþe:
af:bloþ:og:þeþ:AVM:
fräelse:af:illu:
"

Translation: Unlike the version in the infobox above, this is based on Richard Nielsen's 2001 translation of the text, which attempts specifically to put it into a medieval context, giving variant readings of some words:

8 Geats and 22 Norwegians on ?? acquisition expedition from Vinland far west. We had traps by 2 shelters one day's travel to the north from this stone. We were fishing one day. After we came home, found 10 men red with blood and dead. AVM (Ave Maria) Deliver from evils.

The lateral (or side) text reads:

" har:10:mans:we:hawet:at:se:
äptir:wore:skip:14:þagh:rise:
from:þeno:öh:ahr:1362:
"

Translation:

(I) have 10 men at the inland sea to look after our ship 14 days travel from this wealth/property. Year [of our Lord] 1362

Dr. Nielsen's Translation

In order to discover how the runestone and the tower were connected it would be necessary to study the translation by Dr. Richard Neilsen. As previously stated, the builders of the Newport Tower and creators of the Kensington Runestone have little use for words and place most of their emphasis on numbers, geometry and symbols. Attention was directed to the numbers contained in the translation. The above translation is the original translation by Dr. Neilsen. The decoded version follows below.

Text (Nielsen interpretation)
With one slight variation from the Larsson rune rows, using the letter þ (representing "th" as in "think" or "this") instead of d, the inscription on the face (from which a few words may be missing due to spalling, particularly at the lower left corner where the surface is calcite rather than greywacke) reads:

" 8:göter:ok:22:norrmen:po:
??o:opþagelsefarþ:fro
vinlanþ:of:vest:vi:
haþe:läger:veþ:2:skylar:en:
þags:rise:norr:fro:þeno:sten:
vi:var:ok:fiske:en:þagh:äptir:
vi:kom:hem:fan:10:man:röþe:
af:bloþ:og:þeþ:AVM:
fräelse:af:illu:
"

— SUBTRACT 80 DEGREES FROM 093° ORIENTATION OF I.P. TO OBTAIN 13° STARTING POINT.

Translation: Unlike the version in the infobox above, this is based on Richard Nielsen's 2001 translation of the text, which attempts specifically to put it into a medieval context, giving variant readings of some words: *22° @ 2 MILES FROM RUNESTONE SPACER TO I.P.*

8 Geats and 22 Norwegians on '?? acquisition expedition from Vinland far west. We had traps by 2 shelters one day's travel to the north from this stone. We were fishing one day. After we came home, found 10 men red with blood and dead. AVM (Ave Maria) Deliver from evils. *10° @ 22 MILES FROM RUNESTONE TO SPACER*

The lateral (or side) text reads:

" har:10:mans:we:hawet:at:se:
äptir:wore:skip:14:þagh:rise:
from:þeno:öh:ahr:1362:
"

Translation: *100° RADIAL TO BERMUDA* *140° RADIAL TO EAST COAST MARKER*

(I) have 10 men at the inland sea to look after our ship 14 days travel from this wealth/property. Year [of our Lord] 1362 *DISTANCE FROM I.P. TO THREE CORNERS OF U.S.*

Translation Decoded

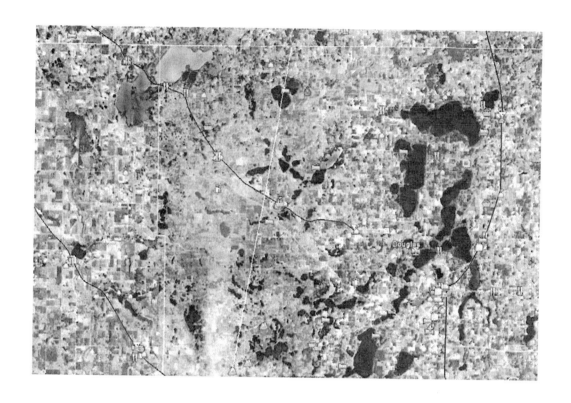

010 Degrees at 22 Miles

One solution derived from the numbers given on the runestone was a heading of 10 degrees at 22 miles. Although this interpretation seemed to be headed in the right direction it still did not give any indication that it was a correct solution to the puzzle. Neither did any of the other combination of numbers. Research was done to see if the method of measurement had changed from 1362 until now. Sure enough Queen Elizabeth had changed the Universal Standard of measurement, the mile, from 5000 feet, before her coronation, to 5280 feet, in 1592, after becoming Queen. That meant that 22 miles in old English miles would convert to 20.8 miles in new English miles. Curiously enough most of the explorer's maps that have been discovered are dated in the 16th Century. Could this change in universal measurement have come about to mask all the measurements done before that.

The Spacer
(46 06 33.05N - 95 35 05.68W)

After converting the English miles the figures 10 degrees at 20.8 miles were used which placed the end point on what became known as "The Spacer". It was called this because the measurements are so precise that if you land on the south end of the spacer and begin your second leg from the south end you will come up short by the same length as the spacer. The second leg of the connection must start on the North end of the spacer. The "Spacer" is the line on the left side of the picture, which looks like a runway, but is in reality a stone wall that someone has mowed around.

Inspiration Peak - 22 Degrees at 2 Miles
(46 08 09.49N 95 34 14.61W)

Now that the Spacer has come into play one must follow the new direction which points (22 Degrees) for two miles from the North end to reach Inspiration Peak. But remember, we are dealing in old English miles so the real distance is 1.9 miles. The end of the last line drawn lands precisely where the West vertex of the Newport Triangle landed.

THE CAMPSITE

The figures displayed above are the figures used to transition from the place where the Kensington Runestone was found, to "Inspiration Peak". However, locating Inspiration Peak was meaningless unless you already knew the geometry associated with it. It appears that the first writer assumed that the reader would already know the geometry and would only need to locate Inspiration Peak in order to apply the mathematics. There was enough information in the first five lines of the text to locate the "...*traps and two shelters one day north from this spot*." (This is referring to a campsite containing the stone wall pointing to Inspiration Peak. This campsite is depicted in the next two photos.) However, the second writer had a different agenda and wanted to make the complete solution available to whoever might find the stone. This would be a prudent move if the second writer assumed the details would be lost to time. But this was not the only reason for placing new information on the stone. Since the time that Inspiration Peak was surveyed, thousands of years before, things had changed that required a revision of the boundaries that had existed for millennia. The cause of that change was the invasion of Mexico by the Spanish explorer Hernando Cortes in 1519. (See photo titled "Revised North American Territory" below)

At the time the Kensington Runestone was first carved, sometime prior to 1592, the Northern Territory had changed. The territory in its original concept included Meso (Central) America and Baja California. In 1519 Hernando Cortes invaded Mexico City and claimed that land for Spain. The New England inhabitants at the time were still too weak to challenge Spain in this action. Besides the Pope had already given North and South America to Spain after the first trip of Columbus. This required an alternative plan. It is believed that this is why the second carving, and the Southern 1362 mile long radial was placed on the stone. This was a quick and easy way to modify the original land claim to fit their current situation. However, this also required a revision to the Kensington Runestone to show the new boundaries and the addition of the Southern 1362 degree radial. The critical addition to the Kensington Runestone was the number 1362. As you will see, below the number 1362, the 110 degree radial and the 140 degree radial were also added and were critical in establishing the revised boundaries of the North American Territory . The new information was a crucial part of revising the ancient survey done in North America thousands of years before. That ancient North American survey was revised to exclude Central America and retain Baja California. Unfortunately Baja California was also lost in the negotiations after the Mexican American war.

Campsite One Day North of Kensington Runestone Site

This photo is presented so that you could see the geoglyphs on the ground before they were covered up in the next photo.

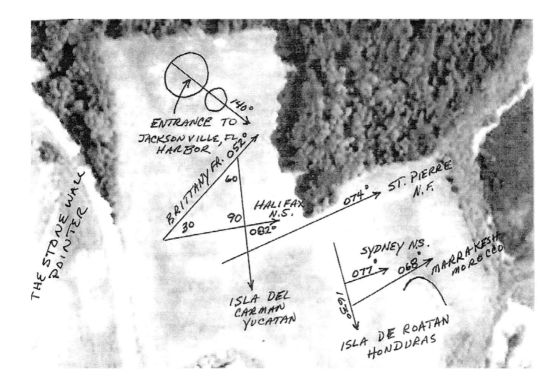

Campsite With Geoglyphs and Stone Wall Pointing to Inspiration Peak

This campsite is obviously the one mentioned in the first five lines on the Kensington Runestone. The stone wall here is oriented 22 degrees at 2 miles from Inspiration Peak. All that would be necessary from here is to follow the stone wall pointer, a common pointer in Geoglyphology at the time, to Inspiration Peak. The Pre-Columbian geoglyphs confirm this was a campsite as placing geoglyphs at your campsite to claim a territory, or denote your travels, was a common practice. The radial endpoints shown in the photo are all known, Pre-Columbian, geoglyphic locations.

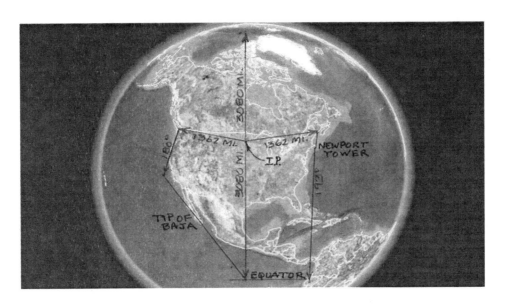

**Inspiration Peak, Minnesota USA - The North American Territory
As Established Sometime Between 10,000 BC and 3150 BC.**

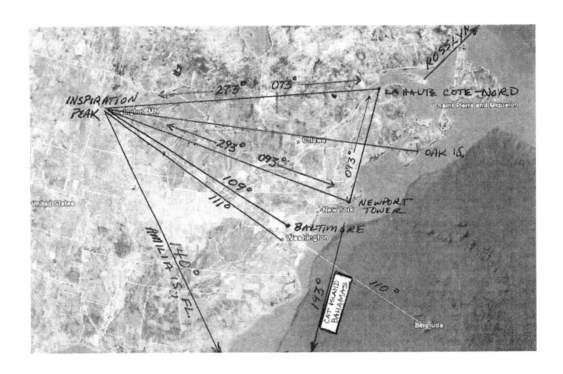

Inspiration Peak Radials as Defined after 1559.

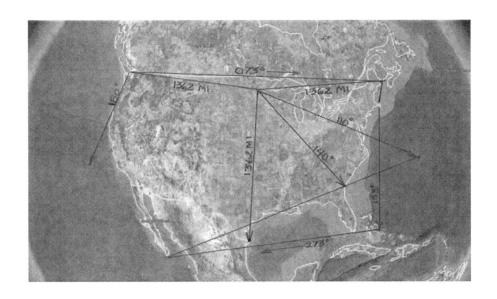

**Inspiration Peak, USA - Revised North American Territory - Circa 1559
After the Spanish Conquest of Mexico in 1515.**

VALIDATION OF THE 1362 MILE LONG RADIALS

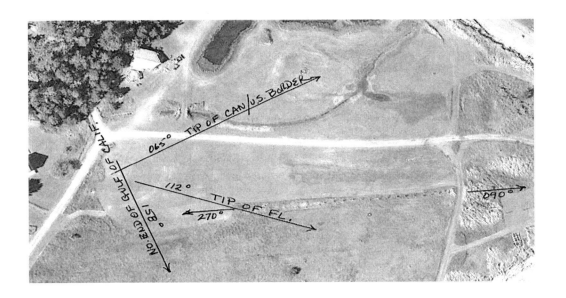

The 1362 Northwest Endpoint and Associated Geoglyph
48 40 26.90N 123 10 11.61W

Depicted above is the termination point of the Northwest 1362 mile long radial from Inspiration Peak. The associated square geoglyph is a survey marker validating the Northeast corner of the Northern Territory. (Later to become the United States.) This geoglyph is on Stuart Island, the last island before Vancouver Island, Canada, and is still within the US borders. Based on protocols used in constructing the four geoglyphs depicted here, it is believed that the geoglyphs were made by the same persons that revised the North American Land Claim. It is apparent that they wanted there to be no mistake as to the territory which they claimed, and as would be proved later, were willing to fight for.

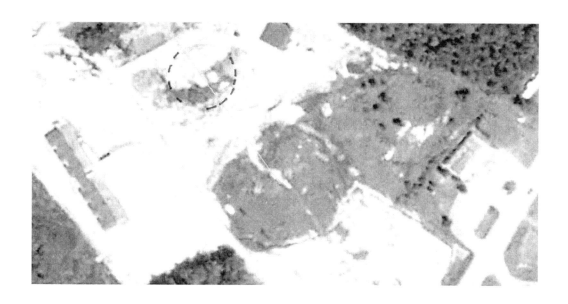

The 1362 Northeast Endpoint and Associated Geoglyph
45 07 57.09N 67 18 56.65W

Depicted above is the termination point of the Northeast 1362 mile long radial from Inspiration Peak. Unfortunately the owners of this property have not taken very good care of this geoglyph. Amazingly, this geoglyph points directly to the island of La Haute-Cote Nord, the island in the Saint Lawrence Seaway that provides the first clue to solving the Newport Tower Puzzle. This geoglyph is located at the original Northern boundary of the State of Maine and the Northern Territory. The land north of here was added later.

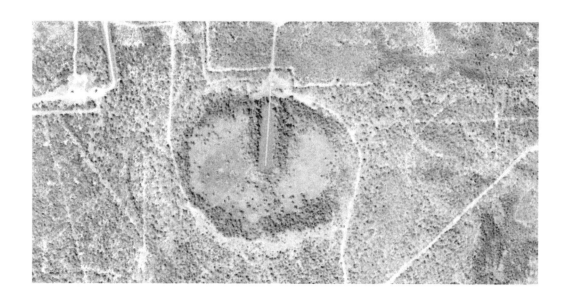

The 1362 Southern Texas Endpoint and Associated Geoglyph #1
26 26 33.42N 97 33 02.47W

This and the next geoglyphs require some explanation. When the Southern
1362 mile long radial was added, after the 1519 invasion of Mexico by
Cortes, it extended to within 30 miles of the Rio Grand River. Although the
Rio Grande is the current Southern Boundary of the United States there is no
reason to think that this spot was not a satisfactory point for the Southern
boundary of the United States circa 1559. Besides as stated before, Spain
had taken over Mexico and claimed that the Rio Grande river was in
Mexico. Therefore, the US claim, by design or fate, stopped 30 miles North
of the Rio Grande. The land between the 30 mile geoglyphs, and the Rio
Grande river, was later won by General Zachary Taylor, later president
Taylor, in the war with Mexico. After winning the land around the Rio
Grand river, General Taylor rebuilt a captured Mexican fort into the Brazos
Island Supply Depot to support Union troops in the Mexican War. That
depot is depicted in the second picture below and is also contains geoglyphs
establishing the new Southern tip of the United States. The geoglyph
depicted above points directly to, and is 1361 miles from, Inspiration Peak.
Since this geoglyph is 1361 miles from Inspiration Peak and the geoglyph
below is 1362 miles from Inspiration Peak it is believed that the geoglyph at
the 1361 mile marker was added later.

**The 1362 Southern Texas Endpoint and Associated Geoglyph #2
26 25 25.62N 97 33 16.16W**

The geoglyph depicted above points directly to, and is 1362 miles from,
Inspiration Peak.

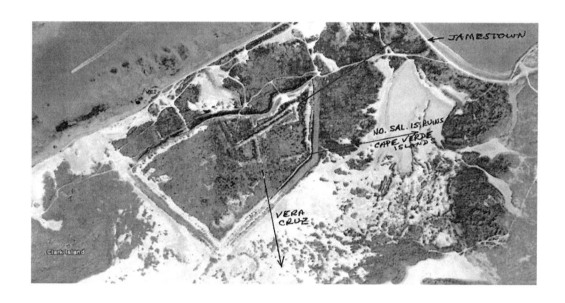

The Brazos Island Supply Depot
26 03 23.77N 97 10 06.76W

This is the Brazos Island supply depot and geoglyphs. Although there are
only three radials depicted in the photo, General Taylor incorporated 18
bearings into the depot that can be measured and followed. There are scores
more that lie outside the depot which outlined the boundaries of the old
North American land claim. There was an attempt to destroy the glyphs
outside the depot but there are enough of them left to measure. They are very
difficult to find unless you know where to look.

THE ALL SEEING EYE

The Inspiration Peak All Seeing Eye
(45 51 03.03N - 95 34 24.55W)

In the preceding photo is the glyph of the "All Seeing Eye" which is seen in Egyptian hieroglyphics, Masonic icons, and on the US one dollar bill. This glyph, and the key next to it, are of raised earth so that they will stand the test of time. This and similar glyphs are located at numerous locations around the United States as survey markers and reminders of European visitations in ancient times. The last glyph known to have been constructed in the USA are the streets of Washington DC. The key glyph to the left of the eye is oriented at 360 degrees true, and points right back to Inspiration Peak.

Well, here is the payoff. Inspiration Peak is indeed a survey marker claiming the choicest part of North America. Please note that not only is the marker equidistant from the equator and the North Pole and the three corners of what is now known as the USA, but that the Northern Corners of the United States are both located on lines of 20 degrees of magnetic deviation. What genius did this survey?

The date of 1362 on the Kensington Runestone, and the erratic carbon dating results, explains why there has been so much confusion over the dating of the Kensington Runestone. As you saw in the runestone presentation the date of 1362 AD is not a date but a measurement, and since it is comprised of miles instituted in 1592, at 5280 feet per mile, shows that it was placed on the stone after 1592. The first five lines were placed there prior to 1592. This is confirmed by the fact that the measurements in the first five lines are calculated in terms of miles comprised of 5000 feet each, the standard in use before 1592.

END CHAPTER

Chapter 11

Portuguese History

The Big Question

Since I first found out that the Vikings came to America, before Columbus, I have labored with the nagging question as to why people, in many countries, refuse to acknowledge this fact. The history preserved regarding Columbus' first trip to America, and his discoveries, are almost comical in comparison to the physical proof that the Vikings preceded him to the Americas by at least 500 years, and others much earlier than that.

Along the trail of research on this book I learned that Portugal had, at some point, aligned itself with Spain. Could this be so? Did the Portugal that I had been championing, along with the other Celtic countries, as a colonizer of the New World changed sides? As I researched the history of Portugal I had my answer.

Celtic Portugal

Man first appeared in what is now Portugal during the Old Stone Age. It is believed they traveled from what is now Southern France prior to 10,000 BC, by entering through the low passageway between the shore and the west end of the Pyrenees. The Celts arrived thousands of years later, and brought a small group of Germans with them. They settled mostly in the north of the Iberian Peninsula, especially in what is now the north of Portugal and the, now Spanish, province of Galicia. Celtic languages spread from Southern France throughout most of the north of Iberia, and extended southward to include central Portugal. The people lived in villages of round stone houses which can still be seen in northern Portugal, and eventually they established contact with their kinfolk in Brittany and the British Isles for the metal trade, which included tin, copper and lead.

A Celtic Round House

These Celts, which came to be known as "Lusitanians," had a similar culture to the groups already in Iberia, which allowed them to settle in peace and cooperation. In certain areas, these Celts mixed with the other population, and created groups that were named "Celtiberians."

Roman Portugal

The Romans overran Gaul (today's France) in seven years, but it took them almost two centuries to completely take over Iberia. The Romans settled everywhere, but their numbers in the North of Iberia was comparatively small. The South was more to their liking, which was better for growing wheat, olives, and grapes. They eventually imposed their language upon the entire peninsula, and their code of law was applied, which was also ultimately the basis of the Portuguese legal code. Forums, temples and law courts were built in the cities, large-scale agriculture was conducted, and the plow was introduced. Roads and bridges (still in evidence throughout Portugal) were created, as well as a system of large farming estates called Latifundios still seen in the area of Alentejo. Under Decimus Junius Brutus and Julius Caesar, a capital was established at Olisipo (Lisbon), and around 25 BC, Augustus Caesar divided the peninsula into several provinces, naming much of the area that eventually became Portugal "Lusitania." During this time the Galicians and Northern Portuguese were integrating themselves into the Roman economy in order to prosper from there new Roman benefactors. This practice of quietly integrating themselves into the fabric of their times would continue and make them very rich from military and mercantile contracts with the Romans and other countries.

Germanic Portugal

The weakening of the Roman Empire enabled various Teutonic peoples to invade Gaul. They eventually crossed the Pyrenees and entered Iberia. The Suevi (or Swabians), who stayed mostly in the northwest, made Bracara Augusta (now the Portuguese city of Braga) their capital. These new German rulers, possibly of Hebrew heritage, did not altogether sweep away Roman civilization, which they had learned to admire. The Germanic groups wore their hair long, while the Romans clipped theirs. However, they blended easily with the Romans, as well as with the Celts, whose culture was not too different from theirs. The great contribution of the Swabians was in the use of land, and the introduction of the quadrangular plow. They preferred to settle in the North and Northwest of Iberia, which are areas that had a climate more suitable to their crops. In 400 AD the Swabians and Galicians invaded Italy and captured Rome.

Moorish Portugal

The Prophet Mohammed preached his new religion, Islam, in Arabia, and when he died in 632 AD, his successors undertook a program of world conquest in the name of Allah and Islam. By 700, their forces swept across North Africa and subdued predominantly Christian Egypt and Morocco. They crossed into what is now Spain in 711, and over the years subjugated almost the entire peninsula with incredible speed. However, as opposed to the previous invaders of Iberia, these Muslims (who were named "Moors" by the Christians), chose to settle mostly in the South. In the area of present Portugal, their presence was stronger mostly in today's Alentejo and Algarve provinces. It was during this period of Moorish conquest that a large contingent of Galicians moved their colonies to what is now known as Denmark. The Galicians, having lost their lucrative Roman contracts and Roman protection, needed a military force to reestablish themselves in their new home. It is believed that it was at this time the Danish Galicians made a pact with the Norsemen to be their military arm. This is precisely the same time (800 AD) that the Vikings, who had not been heard from previously, became a part of history. The Galicians, now the Danes, had grown rich from their dealings with the Roman Empire and their metal mines in Cornwall England and could well afford to fund a military. The Danes military would eventually become known as the Vikings.

About 200 years later cannons were placed on sailing vessels and the time of overpowering your enemy with brute force was over. In addition the political climate was changing in the Baltic to a commerce oriented climate which begin to replace barbarianism and piracy. By 1200 AD when a Baltic non-aggression pact was formed, called the Hansiatic League, the Vikings had disappeared from the North Sea. Having been allocated a portion of the Ancient Celtic Land Claim in North America, by their benefactors the Celts, they begin leaving there mark on their home in the New World.

Christian Re-conquest and the Emergence of Portugal

Christians continuously tried to get rid of the Moors after the Muslim invasion of Europe in 700AD. The first attempt is said to have been as early as ten years after their invasion. This was when a man named Pelagio won the first Christian victory against the hated invaders in the North of Iberia. Though the military significance was small at the time, it lifted Christian morale. Over the years, the Christians re-conquered several areas from the North and the South of the peninsula (the North was re-conquered earlier, with the Portuguese cities of Oporto back in Christian hands by 868 and Coimbra by 1064). Several Christian Kingdoms were formed. In 1095, Alfonso VI, the ruler of the kingdom of Leon and Castile established the County of Portucale between the rivers Douro and Mondego. In 1139, the ruler of this county, Afonso Henriques won a battle over the Moors, and declared Portucale (Portugal) a separate kingdom, with himself as king. Four years later, Alfonso VII of Leon-Castile recognized Portucale as a separate, independent kingdom, as did Pope Alexander III in 1179. Afonso Henriques continued to capture land from the Moors, and by 1147 he re-conquered Lisbon with the help of English, Flemish, German, and French crusaders. Evora was retaken in 1166, and the Algarve in 1249. At this point, Portugal's conquest was complete, and Portugal became Europe's first state to reach the limits of its territorial expansion, which remain unchanged to this day.

The Age of Discovery

After Portugal was able to expel the Moors, neighboring Castile (Spain) tried to do the same, achieving that goal in 1492. But over those years it also tried to take over Portugal. There were several invasion attempts, ending with a Portuguese victory in the Battle of Aljubarrota in 1385, during King Joao's rein. Joao's rein saw Portugal's colonial expansion in Africa and the voyages of discovery which made Portugal rise as the leading maritime and colonial power in western Europe, and saw Lisbon develop into a major commercial city. In 1415 the trading post of Ceuta in Morocco was captured. In 1419, Joao's son, Prince Henry the Navigator begin promoting voyages of discovery by opening his "School of Navigation" in Sagres, Portugal. As a result, the Portuguese were the first Europeans to open the way for massive exploration by training future explorers in navigation.

The Portuguese Navigator's school spelled the end for the secret colonization of the New World by the Celts and their associates. The New World colonists must have felt a deep sense of betrayal by Portugal. It is this betrayal that may be the reason for the destruction of many Portuguese geoglyphs, and the Newport Tower, in the 16th Century, and a refusal to acknowledge that Portugal was in any way connected with the colonization of the Americas. This would also explain a controversy over the age of the Newport Tower in Newport, RI which has been raging ever since the 18th century Colonists first recorded its existence. A carbon dating test of the age of the Newport Tower was done in 1996. (See Appendix B) This report stirred up even more controversy because it showed dates of both 1493 and 1693 AD as possible dates of the construction of the Tower. The destruction of all things Portuguese in the New World in the 16th Century would explain the two dates. The two dates could stem from the Tower being first built in 1493, destroyed in the 16th Century and rebuilt on the Towers 200th Anniversary in 1693.

Thanks to worldwide trade, Portugal enjoyed an upsurge of prosperity, making it the wealthiest country in Europe. Shown below is a Portuguese map of Brazil in 1519. Our research has shown that cities like Rio existed hundreds of years before this map was made. Notice the Celtic Cross on the sail of the sailing ships.

A 1519 AD Portuguese Map of Brazil

In the 15th and 16th centuries, Portugal ascended to the status of a world power during Europe's "Age of Discovery" as it built up a vast empire including possessions in South America, Africa, Asia and the near East. And why not, Portugal already had settlements in all those places. In the next two centuries, Portugal gradually lost much of its wealth and status as the Dutch, English and French took an increasing share of the spice and slave trades (the economic basis of its empire), by surrounding or conquering the widely-scattered Portuguese trading posts and territories, leaving it with ever fewer resources to defend its overseas interests.

Signs of military decline began with two disastrous battles: the Battle of Alcacer Quibir in Morocco in 1578 and Spain's abortive attempt to conquer

England in 1588 (Portugal was then in a dynastic union with Spain and contributed ships to the Spanish invasion fleet). The country was further weakened by the destruction of much of its capital city in a 1755 earthquake, occupation during the Napoleonic Wars and the loss of its largest colony, Brazil, in 1822.

60 Years of Spanish Domination

In the late 16th century, King Sebastiao was determined to take Christianity to Morocco. He rallied a force of 18,000 but was killed in the battle along with 8000 others. His successor, Cardinal Henrique took over the throne. In 1580, when Henrique died, Sebastiao's uncle, Phillip II of Spain, claimed the Portuguese throne. Phillip promised a purely personal union that would leave his new kingdom as independent as before, guaranteed the separation of the two governments, and promised that the Portuguese language and laws should be used in the governance of the country. Phillip's rein lived up to his promise, but under his son and grandson, Spain let the English and the Dutch strip Portugal of valuable foreign possessions, and Lisbon declined as a commercial center with competition from the harbors in England and Holland. This marked the end of Portugal's golden age. In 1640, city fathers staged a well-planned rising in Lisbon and easily overpowered the sentinels guarding public buildings. In the absence of any force capable of suppressing the rising, a new ruler was acclaimed and Portugal was once again a separate, independent nation. Later, a treaty of friendship and commercial cooperation with Britain ensured Portugal's restored independence, but also guaranteed British predominance in Portugal. Two years after the treaty, Portugal's Catherine of Braganza (Braganca), married England's Charles II.

The French Invasion

In 1755 a devastating earthquake shattered Lisbon, killing thousands of people and destroying most buildings. The prime minister at the time, the Marquis of Pombal, directed the rebuilding of the city. By the turn of the century, the country went through better times. Much of Lisbon had been rebuilt, the peasant class was stable, the middle class was prospering, and all presided over by the relatively considerate government of Queen Maria I. At about this time however, events in other European countries threatened Portugal. In France, Napoleon declared a blockade of English trade, and the English responded with a continental blockade. The French insisted that the

Portuguese close their ports to the English, open them to Spanish and French ships and arrest all Englishmen in the country and confiscate their property. Not to meet these demands would result in invasion. Portugal had always had a friendly relationship with England, so the government procrastinated. France and Spain then signed the Treaty of Fountainebleau, which gave Napoleon the right to invade Portugal through Spain. They agreed that after the invasion, Portugal would be divided between France and Spain. The French occupied the country in 1807, and the Portuguese royal family fled to Brazil. About 50,000 French and Spanish troops roved the countryside arresting, killing, plundering and raping as they pleased. In 1808 Portugal got help from the British, their oldest allies. With their help (headed by General Sir Arthur Wellesley), defensive lines were built around Lisbon. When Napoleon reached the fortifications, he retreated. After the war a new constitution was proclaimed and Brazil was given independence. The years that followed were marked by political confusion.

Portugal Today

Today Portugal is a stable country well integrated in the European Union. With the common European monetary system, it is believed that the country will gradually reach a standard of living on a par with the other major European countries. Attention in future years will focus on bringing the country's level of skilled jobs and educational achievements closer to the European average.

In 1998 Lisbon hosted the World Fair Expo 98, leading to major infrastructure and urban regeneration projects. A year later, the country adopted the Euro as its official currency along with ten other countries of the European Union, and in 2004 it hosted the Euro2004 championship. In July 2007 it took over the European Union presidency when EU members signed the Lisbon Treaty which revised the EU's constitutional framework. Portugal is now a country looking to the future, while never forgetting its long, remarkable past.

THE PORTUGUESE NAVAGATORS MONUMENT

After studying the city of Newport, RI USA, reviewing its history, and becoming familiar with its people, it became obvious that the people of Newport, if not Rhode Island, have a clear understanding of their Portuguese history but have been reluctant to speak about it or share it with the outside world. Their reluctance to share this information was an additional indication that all was not well with their relationship with Portugal. However, as has been said many times; "Time heals all wounds". This became evident when our team discovered that in 1988 the City of Newport, in cooperation with the Portuguese Government, installed an elaborate memorial to the Portuguese Navigators who had discovered and colonized the area.

In 1419, Prince Henry started the first school of navigation at Sagres, Portugal. Prince Henry the Navigator was a Portuguese explorer, soldier and prince. Prince Henry sent many expeditions from Portugal and was responsible for Portugal's influence in the Great Age of Exploration. Portuguese explorers were the first to sail the world, even before Columbus. The Portuguese Navigator's School was the first indication that Portugal was breaking from the Portuguese/Celtic alliance, for this would train navigators, including those of Spain, to explore the Atlantic and stop the Celtic monopoly in the New World.

It would be a stretch to believe that the most prominent teacher of navigation in the world just came up with these skills without experience. By this time the Portuguese had sailed, and colonized the entire world for hundreds, if not thousands, of years. It was also about this time that Portugal aligned itself with Spain. Shortly thereafter Spain begin its bloody conquest of the New World. The fact that the Spanish did not try to occupy the New England area would lead one to believe that they knew it was already colonized.

One of Prince Henry's most esteemed students was Miguel Corte-Real. Miguel Corte-Real was a son of Joao Vaz Corte-Real and a brother of explorer Gaspar Corte-Real. Gaspar explored North America first in 1499. In 1500 Gaspar set out again with his nephew Miguel. Gaspar eventually sent Miguel, with two ships, back to Portugal. Following this, Gasper was never heard from again.

In May 1502, Miguel set out on an expedition to search for his brother, but he too disappeared. Strangely enough the ships that were with him returned to Portugal also. The sole surviving brother, Vasco Anes Corte-Real, wanted to sail in search of his brother, but the King of Portugal would not fund such an expedition. In 1912 Edmund B. Delabarre claimed that markings on the Dighton Rock in Massachusetts suggest that Miguel Corte-Real reached New England. The Portuguese Navigators Monument at Newport, RI, USA, also home to the mysterious Newport Tower, is mute testimony that many people in high places believe the same thing. The most logical conclusion is that the Uncle and his Nephew knew about the colonies in North America and decided to live there.

The Portuguese Monument in Newport, Rhode Island USA is the realization of the efforts of Arthur Raposo. This Portuguese-American was born in Fall River, but lived for many years in Middletown, Rhode Island.

In his great desire to pay homage to the great navigator, Miguel Corte-Real, he organized the Miguel Corte Real Committee. Composed of ten Portuguese-American leaders, this committee was created for the purpose of erecting a statue in honor of Miguel Corte-Real somewhere in Newport, RI "The City by the Sea".

With enthusiasm and persistence he negotiated with Rhode Island officials until he secured the best spot in the State of Rhode Island for the monument. The Brenton Point State Park. Raposo first presented his plan to Attorney Robert M. Silva, president of the Portuguese Cultural Foundation. Together with Portuguese Cultural Foundation Executive Secretary, Peter Calvet de Magalhaes, they obtained the cooperation of the National Committee of the Commemorations of the Discoveries of Portugal. From this agreement they developed mutual cooperation between Portuguese and American officials, which eventually led to Portugal offering the Portuguese Discovery Monument as a gift to the American people.

Meanwhile, through the joint cooperation of Governor Edward DiPrete, Portuguese-American Legislators, and the Environmental Department of Rhode Island, over $110,000 was allocated to landscape Brenton Point State Park to ready it to receive all the pieces of the Monument. This amount of money was matched by the Portuguese Government, which expended over $110,000 to build and transport the monument to Rhode Island. Adding the cost of the Interpretive Plaque, the total expense for this Monument reached a quarter of a million dollars.

The Portuguese Discovery Monument was inaugurated in 1988. Arthur Raposo always felt the monument was not complete without its Interpretive Plaque. With the official inauguration, documented below, Arthur Raposo and his many fellow Portuguese Americans can finally say that the realization of their dream is now complete.

Information contained on the Interpretive Plaque:

"The monument before you honors the Portuguese navigators of the Golden Age of Maritime Exploration, which spanned from the early 1400's to the late 1500's. During this era, Portugal was the forerunner in maritime exploration -- both coasts of the United States were discovered and colonized by the Portuguese." (Notice they said both coasts.)

Brenton Point was chosen as the site for this monument because it is very reminiscent of Sagres, the point in southern Portugal where Prince Henry founded his School of Navigation in 1419. It was in Segres Portugal that the maritime data collected over hundreds of years. emanated from the minds of the foremost scholars in mathematics, astronomy, cartography and those that were experts in the compass, the astrolabe, water currents and the winds.

There are eighteen elements in the Portuguese Navigators Monument: the sixteen elements placed in a semicircle are an abstraction of the circular compass rose at Sagres, which is all that remains of Prince Henry's School of Navigation today. The elements are placed in a three-quarter sphere, which symbolizes the three-quarters of the world discovered by the Portuguese navigators in the fifteenth century. (Authors Note: As it turns out the monument was not a random display of elements. Each element points to a specific spot in America where a Portuguese navigator placed a survey marker in the early days, 1200 - 1500 AD, of mapping out the boundaries of what is now the United States.)

The World Sphere of the Monument

The large multifaceted stone marker has been designed to evoke the tradition of explorers leaving behind a marker of their presence. The final element represents an armillary sphere, a navigational instrument which is one of Portugal's most significant and enduring symbols. The sphere was added to the Portuguese flag in 1522 to commemorate Magellan's circumnavigation of the globe, and is still included on the country's present flag."

The Interpretive Plaque was inaugurated on Sunday, June 8th, 1997, at 2PM, sponsored by The Portuguese American Federation, Inc. and the Division of Parks and Recreation of Rhode Island. The main speakers at this event were: President of the U. N. Committee on the Oceans: Dr. Mário Soares, Former

President of Portugal And by the Vice-President of United Nations World Committee on the Oceans: Honorable Congressman Patrick J. Kennedy

In attendance at the inauguration of the Interpretative Plaque: Aida Sousa, Executive Secretary of the Federation, Dr. Luciano da Silva and Dr. Mário Soares, President of Portugal.

The words engraved on the Portuguese Discovery Monument:

On the world sphere:

THIS MONUMENT IS A GIFT TO THE PEOPLE OF THE UNITED STATES OF AMERICA, FROM THE RHODE ISLAND GENERAL ASSEMBLY IN CONJUNCTION WITH THE NATIONAL COMMITTEE OF THE COMMEMORATION OF THE DISCOVERIES OF PORTUGAL AND COMMISSIONED UNDER THE AUSPICES OF THE PORTUGUESE CULTURAL FOUNDATION OF RHODE ISLAND. EDWARD D. DIPRETE, GOVERNOR; RICHARD A. LICHT, LIEUTENANT GOVERNOR. THE MIGUEL CORTE-REAL MONUMENT COMMITTEE. PROJECT: SCULPTOR, CHARLES DE ALMEIDA; ARCHITECT JOÃO SANTA-RITA. DEDICATED JUNE 10, 1988

On the tall pillar:

TO THE MEMORY OF THE NAVIGATORS, MAPMAKERS, EXPLORERS, FLEET COMMANDERS AND THOSE OTHERS WHO ENABLED THE DISCOVERY BY THE PORTUGUESE OF TWO-THIRDS OF THE WORLD.

The Geographical Meaning of the Portuguese Discoveries Monument

by Manuel Luciano da Silva, M. D.

The Compass Rose here at Brenton Point is a modern replica of the one at the Portuguese Nautical School, at Sagres, southern Portugal, founded by Prince Henry the Navigator in 1419. The Portuguese Nautical School became the scientific center of the world for discoveries during XV and XVI centuries.

Brenton Point is the closest spot in the Continental United States of America and to Cabo da Roca, (North of Lisbon) in Portugal, which is the closest point to the European continent. The three-quarter sphere represents the three-quarters of the World discovered by the Portuguese navigators in the XV century. The tall obelisk or land marker has inscribed the names of several Portuguese pioneer navigators.

So you see, even though the Portuguese geoglyphs at Newport RI, and other locations, were destroyed in the 16th Century, the Portuguese finally received the recognition they so richly deserved.

TWO PORTUGUESE GEOGLYPHS

Anyone who doubts that the Portuguese, and their Celtic friends, sailed the globe long before any other Europeans only has to experience these two geoglyphs in order to change their mind. The Celtics marked the entire globe with their survey markers long before any other Europeans, except the Egyptians, knew the world wasn't flat. (A great rumor to keep everyone away from the Americas, don't you think?) If you will remember we discussed in a previous chapter that there are no parallel lines that can be drawn on a sphere. That being so, calculating where two lines of the same degree value will come together and working it into your geoglyph can make quite a statement. Well that is the case with the geoglyphs found at the Northwest corner of the US, in Washington State, and another one 988 miles South in Santa Barbara, California.

The Washington geoglyph, in addition to designating the Northwest corner of the US also points to at least seven other places on the globe. One of the places it points out is the Point Conception geoglyph in Santa Barbara, California. (See Below) Another place it points out is the Southern tip of Portugal. In itself, this is nothing unusual. What is unusual is that the makers of these two geoglyphs have tied them together in a way that shows, without a doubt, who made them and the skill which they possessed.

Both geoglyphs use a 48.5 degree radial which terminate at the Southern tip of Portugal. This ties the explorers their country and the two glyphs together for as long as the glyphs exist. This may not be much longer because the Santa Barbara glyph is already under water. This is testimony to not only the geoglyph's age but also the fact that the world's oceans are rising.

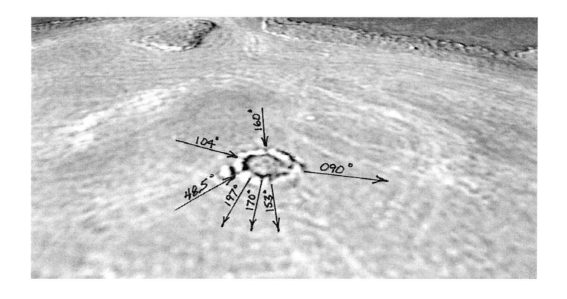

A Second 1362 Northwest Endpoint Geoglyph. This geoglyph is located very near a previously mentioned NW 1362 geoglyph.

Endpoints for the bearings displayed in the above photo.

48.5 Degree Radial - So. Tip of Portugal
090 Degree Radial - Point Lookout, Scotland, MD - Entrance to the Potomac River, USA
104 Degree Radial - Amilia Island, FL - Termination Point of the Inspiration Peak 140 Degree Radial
153 Degree Radial - So. Tip of Baja Mexico
160 Degree Radial - Punta Euginia, Baja Mexico
170 Degree Radial - Point Conception, Santa Barbara, California USA.
197 Degree Radial - Leadbetter Point Glyphs, WA USA - Entrance to Willapa Bay

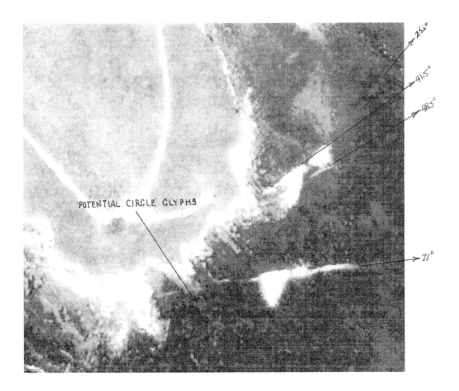

The Point Conception Geoglyph - Santa Barbara, California

Endpoints for the bearings displayed in the above photo.

25.6 Degree Radial - Southern Tip of Norway.

41.5 Degree Radial - North Shore of Galicia at the Southeast corner of the Celtic Empire, as outlined by the 45 degree radials from the Southern tip of Baja, Mexico and the Southern tip of South America.

48.5 Degree Radial - Southern Tip of Portugal. Met by the 48.5 degree radial of the geoglyph in Washington State, USA.

071 Degree Radial - Point Lookout, MD USA - Entrance to the Potomac River.

By combining the major Celtic countries of Norway, Galicia and Portugal in one geoglyph, located 14,200 miles by sea from Portugal, the creator of this geoglyph is making a statement to 21st Century man that should echo around the world.

END CHAPTER

Chapter 12

The Hidden Geoglyphs of Diego Rivera

Diego and Freda Rivera, 1932
Photo by Carl Van Vechten

Diego Rivera was born in Guanajuato, Mexico to a well-to-do family. Rivera
was descended, on his mother's side, from Jews who converted to Roman
Catholicism, and, on his father's side, from Spanish nobility. From the age of
ten, Rivera studied art at the Academy of San Carlos in Mexico City. He was
sponsored to continue study in Europe by Teodoro A. Dehesa Méndez, the
governor of the State of Veracruz. After arrival in Europe in 1907, Rivera
initially went to study with Eduardo Chicharro in Madrid, Spain, and from
there went to Paris, France, to live and work with the great gathering of
artists in Montparnasse.

In those years, Paris was witnessing the beginning of cubism in paintings by
such eminent painters as Pablo Picasso and Georges Braque. From 1913 to
1917, Rivera enthusiastically embraced this new school of art. Around 1917,
inspired by Paul Cézanne's paintings, Rivera shifted toward Post-
Impressionism with simple forms and large patches of vivid colors. His

paintings began to attract attention, and he was able to display them at several exhibitions.

In 1920, urged by Alberto J. Pani, the Mexican ambassador to France, Rivera left France and traveled through Italy studying its art, including Renaissance frescoes. After Jose Vasconcelos became Minister of Education, Rivera returned to Mexico in 1921 to become involved in the government sponsored Mexican mural program planned by Vasconcelos. The program included such Mexican artists as José Clemente Orozco, David Alfaro Siqueiros, and Rufino Tamayo, and the French artist Jean Charlot. In January 1922, he painted his first significant mural Creation in the Bolívar Auditorium of the National Preparatory School in Mexico City while guarding himself with a pistol against right-wing students.

In the autumn of 1922, Rivera participated in the founding of the Revolutionary Union of Technical Workers, Painters and Sculptors, and later that year he joined the Mexican Communist Party. His murals, subsequently painted in fresco only, dealt with Mexican society and reflected the country's 1910 Revolution. Rivera developed his own native style based on large, simplified figures and bold colors with an Aztec influence clearly present in murals at the Secretariat of Public Education in Mexico City begun in September 1922, intended to consist of one hundred and twenty-four frescoes, and finished in 1928.

Rivera's radical political beliefs, attacks on the church and clergy, as well as his dealings with Trotskyists and left-wing assassins made him a controversial figure even in communist circles. Leon Trotsky lived with Rivera and Kahlo for several months while exiled in Mexico. Some of Rivera's most famous murals are featured at the National School of Agriculture at Chapingo near Texcoco (1925–27), in the Cortés Palace in Cuernavaca (1929–30), and the National Palace in Mexico City (1929–30, 1935).

In the autumn of 1927, Rivera arrived in Moscow, accepting an invitation to take part in the celebration of the 10th anniversary of the October Revolution. Subsequently, he was to paint a mural for the Red Army Club in Moscow, but in 1928 he was ordered out by the authorities because of involvement in anti-Soviet politics, and he returned to Mexico. In 1929, Rivera was expelled from the Mexican Communist Party. His 1928 mural "In the Arsenal" was interpreted by some as evidence of Rivera's prior knowledge of the murder of Julio Antonio Mella allegedly by Stalinist assassin Vittorio Vidali. After divorcing Guadalupe (Lupe) Marin, Rivera married Frida Kahlo in August 1929. Also in 1929, the first English-language book on Rivera, American journalist Ernestine Evans's The Frescoes of Diego Rivera, was published in New York. In December, Rivera accepted a commission to paint murals in the Palace of Cortez in Cuernavaca from the American Ambassador to Mexico.

In 1945 Diego Rivera was commissioned to paint the Mural known as Michoacan in the National Palace of Mexico City. Michoacan is a peaceful, yet historical area west of Mexico City. It was from a spot in Michoacan, overlooking Lake Patzcuaro to the Volcano in the distance, that Rivera based the theme of his mural. It is from this same location that the criteria found in the Michoacan mural was applied.

Diego Rivera's Mural "Michoacan Mexico"
National Palace Mexico City, Mexico

**Photo Taken From the Approximate Spot
From Which the Michoacan Mural Was Based**

Michoacan Mural with Radials Depicted

Endpoints of the radials depicted in the Diego Rivera mural of Michoacan, Mexico.

026 Degree Radial – So. Tip of Lake Michigan, USA
027 Degree Radial – Reykjavik, Iceland
033 Degree Radial – So. Tip of Texas, USA
039 Degree Radial – Stonehenge, UK
041 Degree Radial – So. Tip of Newfoundland
043 Degree Radial – Newport Tower, RI USA
044 Degree Radial – Pyramid of Giza, Egypt
048 Degree Radial – Cape Hatterus, Easternmost Point in the US
064 Degree Radial – Canary Islands, Coast of North Africa
079 Degree Radial – No. Tip of Yucatan, Mexico
086 Degree Radial – Anguilla Is., Antilles
087 Degree Radial – Antigua Is., Antilles
089 Degree Radial – Guadalupe, Is., Antilles
090 Degree Radial – Dominica Is., Antilles
091 Degree Radial – Martinique Is., Antilles
129 Degree Radial – Where Equator and Coast of Ecuador meet.
152 Degree Radial – Galapagos Islands, Pacific
161 Degree Radial – So. Tip of South America
298 Degree Radial – So. Tip of Baja California
319 Degree Radial – Glyphs at North End of the Gulf of California
322 Degree Radial – Westernmost Point in the USA
360 Degree Radial – North Pole

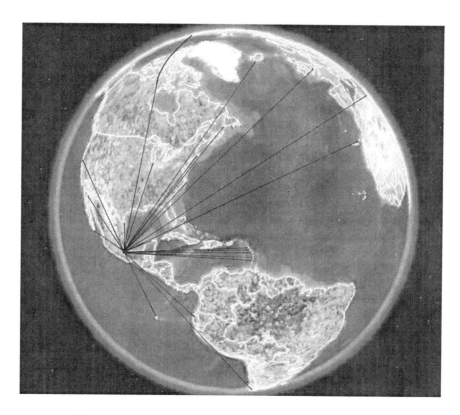

**End Points of Michoacan Radials Plotted Out,
Originating from the Town of Micoacan, Mexico.**

The three panels that are shown below are painted just below the Michoacan Mural. They too contain geoglyphs, which have not yet been plotted. However, these geoglyphs, rather than emanating from straight lines, as the Michoacan radials did, use small circles with dots in the center. These dots are intended to be plotted by laying the panel down flat and running a line through the dots in order to determine a bearing which can be followed to its intended destination.

Michoacan Panel 1

Michoacan Panel 2

239

Michoacan Panel 3

The following two Diego murals have not yet been plotted. However, the possibilities for geometric projections are clearly visible. The projections would be made by extending any straight lines that appear in the murals, or by running a line through two associated round objects in the mural.

Diego Rivera's Mural "The Hauxtex Culture"
National Palace Mexico City, Mexico

Diego Rivera's Mural "Mexico"
National Palace Mexico City, Mexico

DIEGO'S INSIDE KNOWLEDGE

One would have to ask how Diego Rivera obtained the knowledge to paint murals with secret geoglyphs in them. Research, and evidence in this book, indicate that heads of state and their associates have passed down this knowledge for millennium. It has been the basis for territorial agreements and territorial battles. Diego Rivera was the most revered man in Mexico during his time and was associated with heads of state around the world. It would not have been hard for him to have learned this information from them. Whether one of them asked him to incorporate the glyphs in his murals, or whether he did it on his own, remains a mystery.

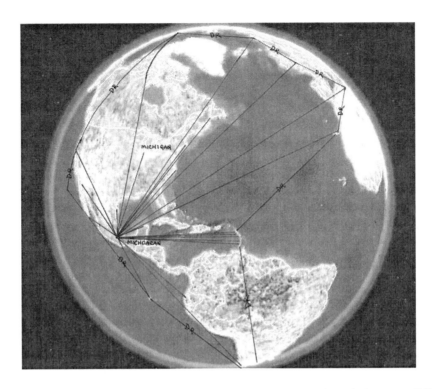

All Encompassing Boundary Projected from Diego's Michoacan Mural

If you will recall the four territorial boundaries outlined in the chapter "The Vikings in America" you will see that there is a common plan that runs through them all. The boundaries outlined in Diego's Michoacan Mural encompass all the territories depicted by the Stonehenge monolith, the Viking geoglyph, the Inspiration Peak survey marker, and the Caral, Peru geoglyph. Further research should more clearly define these boundaries. Study has shown that there are hundreds of smaller geoglyphs, on each continent, which serve to more clearly define the boundaries indicated by the larger geoglyphs. This leaves no doubt that the knowledge for calculating precise radials, over long distances, has existed for millennia and has been unknown by the general public until now.

Although Diego Rivera was a prolific painter, the murals in places of national importance seem to be the only ones which contain secret geoglyphs. I suppose this should be expected since those geoglyphs are ones located in buildings of an international nature.

END CHAPTER

Chapter 13

The Nazca Lines

THE NAZCA PEOPLE

As far back as 1000 BC, the Nazca Valley was inhabited by a people who developed advanced farming methods that allowed them to build an irrigation system, improve their crops, and expand the area of land they could farm. Over the next 1,500 years, they also developed outstanding skills in weaving, pottery, and architecture. The Nazca were wiped out after the Spanish conquest, so that piece of history is quite blank. Perhaps the most fascinating part of their culture is the presence of the remarkable ground art that covers the Nazca Plains.

The Nazca Empire flourished in Peru from about 200 AD to 800 AD before evidence of its existence was lost below the desert sands. Now, large numbers of Nazca graves have been uncovered by both grave robbers and archaeologists. In the fifteenth century, the Inca state expanded from the Cuzco Valley through conquest and assimilation of other cultures. It became the most powerful empire in the New World. But from the time of its expansion the remarkable Inca Empire lasted only around one century before it was destroyed by, the Church sponsored Spanish genocide of Native Americans in the sixteenth century.

However, it is the Nazca lines that draw tourists and scientists to the area. The lines of Nazca are a variety of geometrical figures, trapezoids, triangles and lines, plus animal and bird figures of hummingbirds, a whale, a monkey, a spider, a bird likened to a pelican, another like a condor, and one called the astronaut. They range in size up to 1000 ft (300m) across and are about 2000 years old. The figures on the hills, such as the astronaut, are visible from the ground. The Nazca were potters, like the Moche, and their pottery shows their daily life.

SOCIAL STRUCTURE

Early Nazca society was made up of local chiefdoms and regional centers of power centered on Cahuachi, a non-urban ceremonial site of earthwork mounds and plazas (Valdez, 1994). Scholars have developed theories resulting from various excavations at Cahuachi and suggest that the site was the center for rituals and feasting relating to agriculture, water, and fertility. Cahuachi lies in the lower portion of the Nazca Valley and was initially occupied during the late Paracas phase. It is unique among all other Nazca sites in the region and it is the most important site for the study of ancient Nazca culture (Valdez, 1995). The people modified the natural huacas (hills) into pyramid mounds for ceremonial and religious purposes.

Once more we see a common thread running through the various cultures of the Americas. The Nazca used Mounds in their culture as did the North American peoples (Mississippians) of the same era. The culture was made up of local Chiefdoms surrounded by the associated community, similar to the Mayans. And most important, special ceremonial places were built, apparently away from the normal housing communities that were used exclusively for ceremonial fertility rites. This appears to have begun at least as far back as when the 10,000 year old Yonaguni Pyramid was used. Ceremony and fertility seem to be the focus of many important, ancient archeological sites. Further study needs to be done on this one subject alone.

The material remains found at Nazca sites included large amounts of polychrome pottery, plain and fancy textiles, trace amounts of gold and spondylus shell, and an array of ritual paraphernalia. The remains of pottery found at Cahuachi led archaeologists to believe that the site was specifically non-urban and ceremonial in nature. The ratio of plain, utilitarian pottery to fine, polychrome pottery was 30% to 70% (Silverman, 1988). If it was an urban center, for example, the amount of utilitarian ceramics would have probably been higher. Among the foodstuffs found were maize, squash, and beans; as well as peanuts, and some fish.

PREVIOUS NAZCA STUDIES

The Nazca Lines are a series of ancient geoglyphs located in the Nazca Desert in southern Peru. Some scholars believe the Nazca Lines were created by the Nazca culture between 400 AD and 650 AD. The hundreds of individual figures range in complexity from simple lines to stylized hummingbirds, spiders, monkeys, fish, sharks, orcas, llamas, and lizards. Due to the dry, windless and stable climate of the plateau and its isolation, for the most part the lines have been preserved. Extremely rare changes in weather may temporarily alter the general designs. The Nazca desert is one of the driest on Earth and maintains a temperature around 25 °C (77 °F) all year round. The lack of wind has helped keep the lines uncovered and visible to the present day. This moderate temperature would facilitate the manual labor required to make the geoglyphs.

The lines are shallow designs made in the ground by removing the reddish pebbles and uncovering the lighter ground beneath. Hundreds are simple lines or geometric shapes; more than seventy are designs of animal, bird, fish or human figures. The largest figure is the Star Glyph on the West side of the plain which is 4.33 miles wide. Scholars differ in interpreting the purpose of the designs. They ascribe their purpose as religious, astrological, extra-terrestrial and the list goes on.

After people traveled over the area by plane in the 1930s and saw the Nazca Lines from the air, anthropologists started studying them. Archeologists, ethnologists and anthropologists have studied the ancient Nazca culture, and the complex, to try to determine the purpose of the lines and figures. One theory is that the Nazca people created them to be seen by their gods in the sky. Kosok and Reiche advanced a purpose related to astronomy and cosmology. Many prehistoric indigenous cultures in the Americas and elsewhere constructed earthworks that combined such astronomical sighting with their religious cosmology, as did the later Mississippian culture at Cahokia in present-day United States. Another example is Stonehenge in England. But, Gerald Hawkins and Anthony Aveni, experts in archaeoastronomy, concluded in 1990 that there was insufficient evidence to support such an astronomical explanation.

In 1985, the archaeologist Johan Reinhard published archaeological, ethnographic, and historical data demonstrating that worship of mountains and other water sources predominated in Nazca religion and economy from ancient to recent times. He theorized that the lines and figures were part of religious practices involving the worship of deities associated with the availability of water, which directly related to the success and productivity of crops. He interpreted the lines as sacred paths leading to places where these deities could be worshiped. The figures were symbols representing animals and objects meant to invoke the gods' aid in supplying water. But, the precise meanings of many of the individual geoglyphs remain unsolved as of 2011.

Henri Stierlin, a Swiss art historian specializing in Egypt and the Middle East, published a book in 1983 linking the Nazca Lines to the production of ancient textiles which archeologists have found wrapping mummies of the Paracas culture. He contended that the people may have used the lines and trapezes as giant, primitive looms to fabricate the extremely long strings and wide pieces of textile that are typical of the area. By his theory, the figurative patterns (smaller and less common) were meant only for ritualistic purposes.

Some individuals propose alternative theories. Jim Woodmann believes that the Nazca Lines could not have been made without some form of manned flight to see the figures properly. Based on his study of available technology, he suggests that a hot air balloon was the only possible means of flight. To test this hypothesis, Woodmann made a hot-air balloon using materials and techniques which he understood were available to the Nazca people. The balloon flew, after a fashion. Most scholars have rejected Woodmann's thesis as ad hoc, because of the lack of any evidence of such balloons.

Swiss author Erich von Däniken suggests the Nazca lines and other complex constructions represent higher technological knowledge than he believes existed when the glyphs were created. Von Däniken maintains that the Nazca lines in Peru are runways of an ancient airfield that was used by extraterrestrials mistaken by the natives to be their gods.

Maria Reiche's protégé Phillis Pitluga, an astronomer at the Adler Planetarium & Astronomy Museum, believes, based on computer aided studies of star alignments, that the giant spider figure is an anamorphic diagram of the constellation Orion. She further suggests that three of the straight lines leading to the figure were used to track the changing declinations of the three stars of Orion's Belt but does not take into account the other twelve lines.

Aveni has commented on her work, saying; "I really had trouble finding good evidence to back up what she contended. Pitluga never laid out the criteria for selecting the lines she chose to measure, nor did she pay much attention to the archaeological data Clarkson and Silverman had unearthed. Her case did little justice to other information about the coastal cultures, save applying, with subtle contortions, Urtons representations of constellations from the highlands." As historian Jacquetta Hawkes might ask: was she getting the Pampa she desired?

Up to this point the information supplied to the scientific community and the public has been theory, speculation, and conjecture. As you may have already guessed this book hesitates to present information unless it is accompanied by physical proof, verified history or the surrounding circumstances. I believe you will find them all present in this presentation concerning the Nazca Lines.

THE NAZCA GEOGLYPHS

For almost a Century modern man has marveled at the Nazca geoglyphs, especially the animals, and wondered why they were placed there. The fact is that they are survey markers serving the same purpose as the linier geoglyphs, but with a little more flair. Most people that are familiar with Nazca know of the Hummingbird geoglyph. Due to it's simplicity it was picked to demonstrate the application of Geoglyphology to a non-linier object. Many people might think that the precision required to layout such closely aligned radials does not exist. Let me assure you that it does today in the form of the "Google Pro Software". The ability also existed in ancient times in ways we have yet to discover. One theory is that the ancient's obsession with the alignment of the stars gave them the precision they needed to plot accurately over long distances.

The Nazca Humming Bird Geoglyph

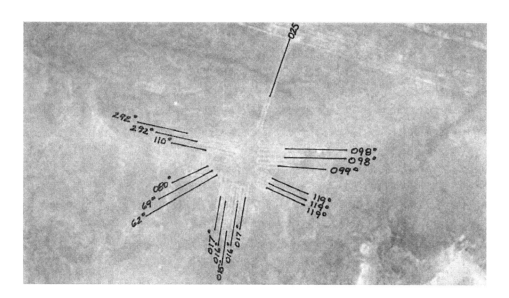

The Nazca Humming Bird Radials

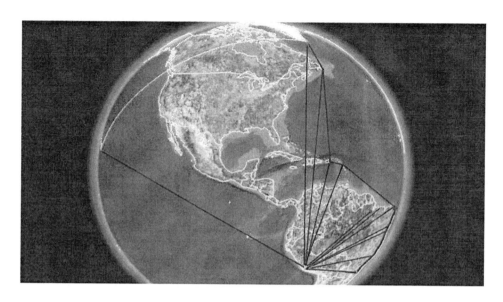

The Territory Formed by the Hummingbird Geoglyph

Endpoints for the bearings displayed in the above photo.

015 Degree Radial - East Tip of Newfoundland.
016 Degree Radial - East Tip of Puerto Rico.
017 Degree Radial - Southern Tip of Greenland.
025 Degree Radial - Dominica Island, Dutch Antilles.
062 Degree Radial - West Tip of Mexiana Island, Brazil - Entrance to the Amazon River.
069 Degree Radial - Isla de Los Lenco, Brazil - Entrance to Triacu Bay.
080 Degree Radial - East Tip of South America.
098 Degree Radial - Fora Island Reef, Brazil – Ent. to Porto Seguro Bay.
099 Degree Radial - Caravelas Point, Brazil - Entrance to Barra River.
110 Degree Radial - Rio de Janeiro Bay, Brazil.
119 Degree Radial - Entrance to Babitonga Bay, Brazil.
292 Degree Radial - Hawaiian Islands.

If you will notice the Portuguese territory generated from the Hummingbird geoglyph, with the exception of Hawaii, matches identically with the combined Viking, North American and South American geoglyphs mentioned in previous chapters. The territories claimed by the Portuguese geoglyphs, on the Nazca Plateau, would be territories that were discovered and claimed prior to Spain's Conquest in the America's beginning c1500 AD.

The Nazca Star

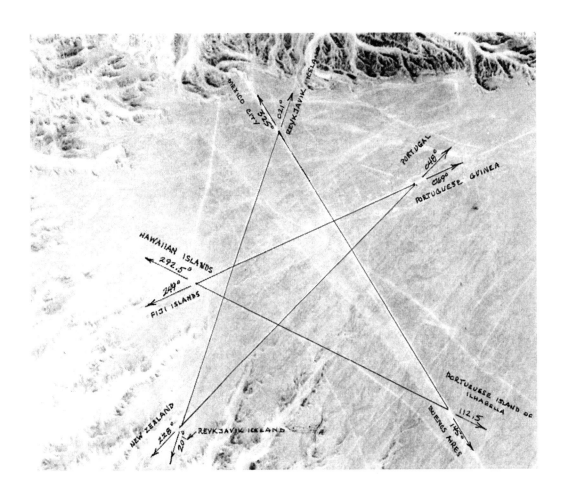

The Nazca Star with Radials Assigned

The Nazca Star geoglyph reflects a Portuguese territory broader than the Hummingbird geoglyph and so it would be logical to assume that it was placed there at a later date. The next geoglyph appears to have been placed about the same time as the Star geoglyph. My estimation would be in the 15th Century just before the Spanish arrived. After the Spanish arrived in South America, Portugal, now aligned with Spain instead of the Celts, shared South America by moving to the Eastern half of South America, particularly Brazil.

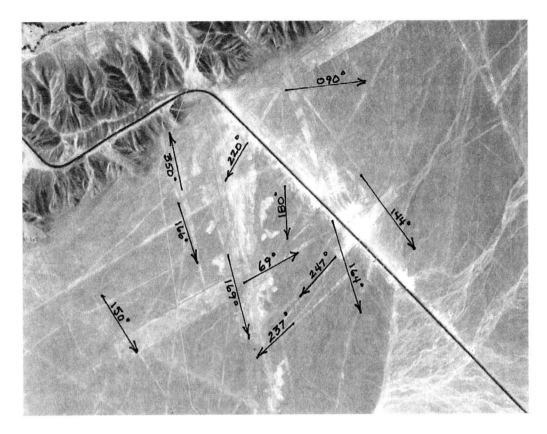

A Later Nazca Geoglyph Decoded

Endpoints for the bearings displayed in the above photo.

069 Degree Radial - Portuguese Guinea, Africa.
090 Degree Radial - Orientation Radial.
144 Degree Radial - Buenos Aires, Argentina.
150 Degree Radial - Zavodovski Island, Northern Island of the 7 South Sandwich Islands.
164 Degree Radial - West Tip of East Falkland Island.
166 Degree Radial - West Tip of West Falkland Island.
169 Degree Radial - Southern Tip of South America.
180 Degree Radial - Orientation Radial.
220 Degree Radial - New Zealand.
237 Degree Radial - Southern Tip of Australia.
247 Degree Radial - Fiji.
350 Degree Radial - Shortest Distance across Panama and boundary between the North and South American land claims.

If you will compare the endpoints of the radials in each of the two preceding Nazca geoglyphs you will notice that there are four endpoints that are repeated in both. Since these two geoglyphs are 73 miles apart it should be obvious that they are not part of the same geoglyphical complex, but were made by persons that had the same experiences and territorial boundaries in mind. There are hundreds, if not thousands, of geoglyphs scratched into the Nazca plateau. It is obvious that they do not all conform to the geoglyphical criteria set out at the beginning of this book. Geoglyphs have been used by mariners and explorers for over 10,000 years all over the world. It would be safe to assume that this valley has been used for the same length of time, or longer, as evidenced by the Caral, Peru geoglyphs. Our research has shown that many of the older geoglyphs we have studied elsewhere were focused on a more local theme. Since colonies and cities have come and gone over the centuries it may be impossible to determine where many of the older Nazca geoglyphs were intended to terminate.

PORTUGUESE LANGUAGE DISPURSAL

The following information, on the dispersal of Portuguese language, is presented to validate the Nazca geoglyphs which appear in the photos above. It is our contention that the geoglyphs were constructed by the Portuguese and their associates during their explorations in pre-Columbian times. As you may have noticed, most of the indicators point to colonies settled by the Portuguese. As may have been mentioned before, Galicia and Portugal share common boundaries and were the first countries established in Europe. The Portuguese language is said to have originated in Galicia, the place of origin of the Danes before they moved North. During the centuries of exploration, immediately preceding Columbus, the Celtics, Galicians and the Portuguese were the primary visitors to the New World. During this pre-Columbian time of exploration the Celtic states of Galicia and Portugal had a great influence on the colonization and resulting languages in many parts of the world. As you read further you will see that several of the places indicated in the two preceding Nazca geoglyphs are also mentioned as speaking the Portuguese language today. Based on the indicators on the Star geoglyph, and the current language spoken in those settlements, it can be deduced that the Celts played a major part in the colonization of these areas.

Without the evidence revealed by the Nazca geoglyphs, one could ask whether the area was settled during pre-Columbian or post-Columbian times. The geoglyphs support the pre-Columbian time period.

Portuguese is the official and first language of Angola, Brazil, Cape Verde, Guinea-Bissau, Mozambique, Portugal, São Tomé and Príncipe. Uruguay gave Portuguese an equal status to Spanish in its educational system at the north border with Brazil. In the rest of the country it's taught as an obligatory subject beginning by the 6th grade. It is widely spoken, though not official, in Paraguay and South Africa.

With more than 200 million native speakers, Portuguese is one of the few languages spoken in such widely distributed parts of the world, and is the fifth most-spoken first language in the world. It is spoken by about 190 million people in South America, 17 million in Africa, 12 million in Europe, 2 million in North America, and 0.61 million in Asia. Portuguese is the third most spoken European language. Portuguese is the most widely spoken language in South America and it is also a key language in Africa.

Portugal, along with Galicia, is the birthplace of the language, which developed from the popular Latin brought there by the Romans in the aftermath of the Punic Wars. A strong Romanization policy, planned by Roman Emperors such as Caesar Augustus, eventually led to the complete extinction of all the former native languages.

There is controversy on whether Galician is within the Portuguese language or if it is a different, although very closely related, language. Spanish administration considers Galician and Portuguese to have had the same origin and common literary tradition. Galician reintegracionists and organizations such as AGAL support the idea that Galician and Portuguese still are the same language, despite some differences. As a matter of fact, spoken Galician was accepted as Portuguese in the Parliament of the European Union and used as such by, among others, the Galician representatives José Posada, Camilo Nogueira and Xosé Manuel Beiras. The international linguistic community generally tends to group them in the same diasystem.

Using language as one indicator of migration and diffusion is a growing, and widely accepted, concept.

END CHAPTER

Chapter 14

HERNANDO CORTES
The Game Changer

BACKGROUND

At the time Cortes invaded Mexico a North American land claim existed that was formed thousands of years before. This claim considered what is now the United States and Central America as one territory. It is a little known fact that the founding fathers had a vested interest in Central America before the War with Mexico in 1846. The land claim, part of which would later become the United States was, slowly and secretly, being populated by the Celts and their predecessors.

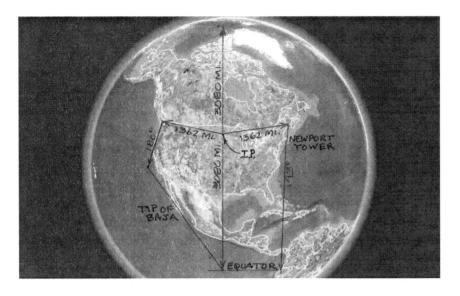

**Inspiration Peak, Minnesota USA - The North American Territory
As Established Sometime Between 10,000 BC and 3150 BC.**

Unfortunately the interests of the Celtic coalition were interrupted when Hernando Cortez invaded Mexico in 1519. The colonists of North America had no standing army and were forced to watch as Spain invaded a land which, for millennia, had been considered part of their North American land claim. The colonists, while not having a fully formed military force, would bide their time in hope that someday they could remedy this invasion by Spain. By the time the Mexican American War begin in 1845, Spain had annexed the entire Western portion of what was planned to be the USA. President Polk, who knew of the original plan to form a country from "sea to shining sea", insisted that we go to war with Mexico and reclaim our land. He called it our "Manifest Destiny" to occupy this land. What follows is a brief history of the beginning of the Mexican American War, the last battle of the Civil War, and the attempt to destroy survey markers on Brazos Island that would could have been used, by either side, to connect Mexico and North America as one contiguous country.

HERNANDO CORTEZ

It was 1504 that a man named Hernando Cortez arrived in what is now known as Cuba. Through his good work he eventually became Mayor of the Capitol of Cuba. In 1518 the Governor of Cuba, Diego Velazquez, put him in command of an expedition to explore and secure the interior of Mexico for colonization. At the last minute, Velázquez changed his mind and revoked his charter. Cortes ignored the orders, to stand down, and proceeded anyway. In February 1519, in an act of open mutiny, and accompanied by about 11 ships, 500 men, 13 horses and a small number of cannons, he landed in the Yucatan Peninsula in Mayan territory. It is no accident that Cortes knew that Vera Cruz was the gateway to Mexico City. This had been known by the Celts for hundreds of years and had been learned by the Catholic Church shortly before Columbus made his first voyage to the Americas in 1492.

In July 1519, Cortez and his men took Vera Cruz. By this act, Cortes dismissed the authority of the Governor of Cuba and, as history claims, went against the orders of the rulers of the Spanish Empire. In order to eliminate any ideas of retreat, Cortes scuttled and burned his ships. In October 1519, Cortes and his men, accompanied by about 3,000 Tlaxcalteca natives, marched to Cholula, the second largest city in central Mexico. Cortés, either in a pre-meditated effort to instill fear upon the natives waiting for him at

Tenochtitlan or (as he later claimed when under investigation) wishing to make an example when he feared native treachery, infamously massacred thousands of unarmed members of the nobility gathered at the central plaza, then partially burned the city. This pattern of inhumanity would repeat itself, over and over, in the Spanish conquest of the Americas. Needless to say this act eliminated any future coalitions the United States might have with the inhabitants of Mexico. Whether Cortez was acting in his own interests or in the interests of Spain may never be known. However it is known that, after Columbus returned from his first voyage to the Caribbean, the Pope decreed that all land west of Africa belonged to Spain. This invasion of Mesoamerica placed a large kink in the plans of the colonizers of the North American Territory. There now existed survey markers on Brazos Island Mexico that outlined the US and Mesoamerica as one country. These survey markers could be used by either side to verify a claim to North and Central America, and they were in Spanish held territory.

Spain begin a campaign to capture as much land as possible before the future US was strong enough to stop them. Eventually they occupied most of the land between Texas and the Pacific Ocean. France also decided to test the Colonies resolve by colonizing the land between the Spanish claim and the Mississippi River. Neither of these countries were members of the secret North Sea Coalition of the Celts.

THE GEOGLYPHS of BRAZOS ISLAND, TEXAS

Brazos Santiago Supply Depot in South Texas

Brazos Island is a barrier island on the Gulf Coast of Texas in the United States, South of the town now named South Padre Island. The island is also known as Brazos Santiago Island, a reference to the town of Brazos Santiago, the first Spanish settlement on the island. The area was granted by the State of Tamaulipas to Ygnacio Trevino on January 24, 1829, as part of the Potrero de San Martin land grant. (The San Martin land grant was granted earlier by the King of Spain.) The island is the southernmost barrier island in Texas, separated from the delta landmass of the Rio Grande by unnamed channels. The island's northern end is separated from South Padre Island by the channel known as the Brazos Santiago Pass. The island is oriented generally north-south, with the Gulf of Mexico on the east, and South Bay on the west. In the course of the natural processes of erosion and sedimentation, the island is not always surrounded by water, and is currently connected to the mainland. A portion of Brazos Island is now designated as a Texas State Scenic Park, also known as Brazos Island State Recreation Area. The beach at this state park is known as "Boca Chica Beach."

BRAZOS SANTIAGO, TEXAS

The first recorded inhabitants of Brazos Island were the Mexicans. The Mexicans established the original Fort Brazos Santiago, a Mexican customs house and military outpost at the entrance to Brazos Santiago Pass. (Across from the Southern tip of Padre Island.) Before 1848 the port had wharves on the lagoon side of Brazos Island. Goods destined for ports up the Rio Grande had to be off loaded at Brazos Santiago because the bars at the mouth of the Rio Grande were too shallow for ships capable of sailing the Gulf. Trade for Matamoros and interior Mexico was landed at the harbor on Brazos Island and then transported to Matamoros by oxcart. In 1840 the government of the Republic of Texas debated the construction of a fort on the north end of Brazos Island, exactly where the Mexicans established Brazos Santiago, six miles north of the mouth of the Rio Grande river. This installation would not only have controlled navigation through the vital pass between Padre and Brazos islands, but would also have established a Texas military presence in the disputed territory between the Rio Grande and the Nueces Rivers. However, since the site lay 120 miles to the south of the nearest Texan settlement, only nominally in disputed Texas territory, and on the site already occupied by the Mexican army, the planned Union fort never materialized

Sometime prior to 1846 a Mexican garrison was established on the site where the current remains of the Union's Supply Depot exists. In March 1846 the Mexican fort was abandoned when the Mexican Commander received word that General Zachary Taylor, later to be President Taylor, and two brigades consisting of 2400 men, with cannon, were headed his way. In 1849 the Fort became Brazos Island Depot, a U.S. Army arsenal and encampment protecting the inlet to Port Isabel and Fort Polk. The fort became a marine transfer station, required to transfer cargo from deep draft ships to shallow draft ships, to supply Forts Polk and Brown. During the Mexican War Gen. Zachary Taylor established a supply depot on Brazos Island, which handled all logistics concerning northern Mexico supplies and men, and where several thousand American troops debarked and waited for assignments to other locations. After 1848 Richard King developed shallow-draft steamboats that could negotiate the shallow bars at the mouth of the Rio Grande. His boats could then offload in the lee of Brazos Island, go around to the Gulf side, and cross the bars and travel up the Rio Grande to their destination. A road was built down Brazos Island, across Boca Chica Bay to the Rio Grande in 1846. To cross Boca Chica Bay, General Zachary Taylor built a floating bridge to transport military supplies. Some of the Cypress pilings are still visible. In 1846, General Ulysses S. Grant crossed here returning from the fighting in Mexico. In 1847, Robert E. Lee crossed the tract similarly several times.

FORT POLK

In 1846, with the heightening of international tension after the annexation of Texas to the United States, Maj. Gen. Zachary Taylor's army marched to the Rio Grande and established itself opposite Matamoros, from where it drove the Mexican garrison at Brazos Santiago back across the Rio Grande, while converting the Mexican installation to an arsenal. On March 6 Taylor's men established a military depot near the Brazos Santiago arsenal (In Port Isabelle just to the North of the current approach to the South Padre bridge.) and named it Fort Polk, in honor of the president of the United States. Fort Polk was garrisoned from 1848 until 1850 by Capt. F. C. Hunt's company of the Fourth United States Artillery regiment. By January 1849, however, the buildings were being moved to different locations on the Rio Grande, and on February 9, 1850, the post was abandoned. The location was used as a transit depot for materials for Fort Brown in 1852, and on February 21, 1861, at the outbreak of the Civil War, it was seized by a confederate artillery company from Galveston. Long afterward, the United States Army Corps of Engineers straightened the channel and installed jetties in the pass, obliterating the site of Fort Polk.

After the Civil War started, in February 1861, Brazos Santiago was occupied by CSA forces where they built a shore battery. The Fort was occupied by the Union from November 1863 until July 1864 while Brownsville was occupied. The Fort was again occupied by the CSA until recaptured by the Union again in 1865 just before the war ended. On September 6, 1864, Colonel H. M. Day and troops marched from Brazos Santiago across Boca Chica Bay to White's Ranch, opposite Tamaulipas, attacked Confederate forces under Captain Richard Taylor and forced their retreat to Brownsville. On September 9, Lieutenant Daniel Showalter attacked federal forces at Palmito Hill. Colonel Day and a Mexican force drove them back again to Brownsville. On May 11, 1865, 300 Union soldiers marched down Brazos Island, across Boca Chica Bay, and attacked White's ranch the next morning.

Confederate forces counterattacked at Palmito Hill and the federal troops were driven back to Boca Chica Bay. The Battle at Palmito Hill was the last battle of the American Civil War. By 1867 the north end of Brazos Island was a well-developed military port with three wharves on Brazos Santiago Pass, a railroad south to Boca Chica and on to Whites Ranch on the Rio Grande, four barracks, a hospital with four outbuildings, two gun emplacements, numerous warehouse buildings, and a lighthouse. After the Civil War the troops left Brazos Island, and the small town of Brazos faded away; most of the buildings were destroyed by the hurricane of 1867.

BIBLIOGRAPHY: Southwestern Historical Quarterly, Texas Collection, July 1943, January 1945. (Writers' Roundtable, Padre Island, San Antonio: Naylor, 1950)

MEXICAN-AMERICAN WAR

In May 1845 Taylor was ordered to correspond with the government of the Republic of Texas, then negotiating annexation to the United States, and to repel any invasion by Mexico. In July he moved his army of 4,000 men to the site of Corpus Christi, Texas. In January 1846 he was ordered to the mouth of the Rio Grande to support the American claim of the river as the boundary of Texas. In March he constructed Ft. Brown, opposite the Mexican town of Matamoros

United States President James K. Polk, who envisioned a nation stretching to the Pacific Ocean, had been elected the year before. Much of the territory he sought to reclaim had been settled by Mexico. The land consisted of what is now the states of New Mexico, Arizona, and California. Polk hinted that if Mexico wouldn't sell these territories, the United States would seize them. He also championed Texas's claim to a southern border along the Rio Grande. The issues of western expansion and the disputed Texas border became intertwined.

"Manifest Destiny" was a popular slogan of the day, reflecting a view that the United States was destined to control the land between the Atlantic and Pacific oceans. Bolstered by such sentiments, Polk sent an emissary to Mexico in an attempt to buy the Western lands. When Mexican officials rejected the offer, Polk ordered U.S. troops, led by General Zachary Taylor, to invade the disputed region between the Nueces and Rio Grande rivers. The president was knowingly courting war. If bloodshed erupted, however, he wanted Mexico to be perceived as the aggressor. Having United States forces in the disputed region increased the likelihood that Mexican troops would cross the Rio Grande and strike the first blows. Powerful voices in the United States spoke against Polk's provocations, including John Quincy Adams, a former president; John C. Calhoun, a former vice president; and philosopher Henry David Thoreau.

When Mexican forces attacked his troops, Taylor did not wait for Congress to declare war. On May 8, 1846, at Palo Alto, he defeated a Mexican army three times the size of his own force, largely through the accuracy of his artillery. The next day he won the Battle of Resaca de la Palma and then occupied Matamoros. President James K. Polk thereupon named him commander of the Army of the Rio Grande and promoted him to Brevet Major General. A grateful Congress voted him thanks and two gold medals

What history has not told us is that President Polk had good reason to lay claim to the land between Texas and California, which the Mexicans had already begin occupying. Thousands of years before this time, a civilization yet to be named, had laid down a series of territorial land claims. One of the land claims contained what is now the United States and Central America. At the time Cortes invaded Mexico this land was being populated by the people of a Celtic, North Sea Coalition. The coalition must have realized that they could not defend the vast area of Central and North America with no established military force. Therefore, it is apparent, that they decided to wait until the time was appropriate to reclaim this land.

The apparent members of the North Sea Coalition were Scotland, Norway, Holland, Galicia, Portugal, Denmark and, prior to the Muslim invasion c700 AD, Egypt. Other Celtic areas participated such as Cornwall, Wales, Britannia and Ireland. Even though, in 1493, the Pope had given both North and South America to Spain, the coalition was successful in maintaining a presence in Eastern North America. It is interesting that the first landing of Columbus was at the precise point where the Celtic North and Spanish South portions of the revised land claim was divided. It is speculated that Columbus came to the New World, not to discover it, but to divide it.

All this was to the exclusion of England which was at war with one or all of them at one time or another. Eventually, Holland received the Netherland Antilles a small part of South America, and exclusive rights to trade in Asia. Spain received the better part of the Caribbean Islands and the Western half of South America. Portugal received the Eastern half of South America with small concessions to Holland and France to establish ports in South America. France, who was also left out of the original agreement, colonized Southeast Canada and eventually the land called the Louisiana Purchase. England had been at war with the participating countries and was not part of any agreement. Later, when England realized what had happened they tried colonizing the New World, thereby evoking a Revolutionary War. The Plate below illustrates the territories involved in the Celtic North Sea Coalition. This territory evolved to include Iceland, Greenland, Eastern Canada, Newfoundland, Nova Scotia, and Eastern North America.

This Map Shows the Countries and Territory Occupied by a Coordinated Celtic Empire c800 AD.

The next Plate illustrates the division of South America as the result of the Portuguese alignment with Spain. One might wonder how seven countries could agree on something as important as a land acquisition; much less keep it secret for hundreds of years. After studying the illustration, and consulting the history books, it will become clear that the countries involved, tightly joined by marriage and purpose, could have made an agreement as to how to divide up the New World. Once the agreement was made it was to everyone's benefit to keep the secret. Each of the participating countries would benefit from the unlimited resources of the new world. Another indication that there was an agreement was the fact that the Pope had given all of the land West of Africa to Spain in 1493. Is it not reasonable to assume Spain would have fought for all of North and South America if some agreement had not been reached in secret, to the exclusion of England, the enemy of all the participants.

It was not until Cortez invaded Mexico and the English and other Europeans begin colonizing the Americas that the whole thing unraveled. Cortez may have thought he had good reason for conquering Mesoamerica for Spain. Portugal and Galicia had colonized the East coast of South America long before Spain even knew the continent existed. However, the only access to the West coast of South America was a long and dangerous journey around the Southern tip, or across Central America, part of the ancient Celtic North American land claim and an area flush with Mayan gold. This combined with the only access to their land being through the North American land claim may have given him reason to conquer Mesoamerica. All this combined with his thirst for gold made Mesoamerica a prize for Spain. The history books report that Cortez invaded Mesoamerica against orders. It may never be known whether Spain had secretly ordered Cortes to invade Mexico. Regardless, it was a strategic move for Spain.

South American Land Division

It is not surprising that France too may have later thought that they had been taken advantage of in any North American land division. France would have found out that Canada was too cold to be of any great value as a colony. There was no doubt that the Celtic colonists had seized the prized land for themselves. But why not, they had surveyed and colonized the land even before the other countries knew about the Americas. This may have caused France to claim the land known later as the Louisiana Purchase. The Nordics were now in a tight spot. They could not confront the more powerful countries of Spain, France and England so they would have been forced to play a waiting game until they had built their country strong enough to take back the land that they believed was rightfully theirs.

The colonies first test was their move to reincorporate the land known as the Louisiana Purchase back into the US. A conflict was avoided by the purchase of the occupied land from France in 1810. This left the British sandwiched between the newly acquired Louisiana Purchase and the Colonies. During this period the British were stirring up the Indians along the Mississippi and Ohio Rivers against the Colonists. This provided the Colonies with their second international test and resulted in the war of 1812. The war ended in 1815 by the British being defeated at New Orleans. With the first two tests successfully behind them there was only one obstacle remaining in the United States grasp of what they called "Manifest Destiny", Mexico's occupation of the land between Texas and the Pacific Ocean. That led to the third and final test of the new countries strength and resolve, the Mexican-American War. The US had offered to purchase the land occupied by Mexico but they rejected the offer. By now, the fact that Spain had occupied over half of the land that Polk considered as belonging to the United States, had to be putting a dent the Polk's plan of "Manifest Destiny".

This brought up another problem. The survey markers at Fort Brazos, which outlined the North American land claim and joined Central and North America, were now working against them. Did the government occupying North America have claim to Central America, or did the government occupying Central America have claim North America? This prompted the destruction of the Brazos Island survey markers by either Mexico or the US. Where the old markers indicated that North and Central America were combined new markers were needed to outline the new boundaries forced upon the US. This is one reason why there was such a scramble to connect the East and West coasts by rail. It was necessary strategically, legally and economically to protect the US interests.

Enter General Zachary Taylor. General Taylor was sent to Brazos Island, not only to defend the US border against Mexico, but also to change the survey markers on Brazos Island to display the new borders of the United States. Brazos Island, being strategically located between North and Central America, contained a vast array of geoglyphs and was the most important, and comprehensive survey marker site in the Americas. During the Mexican-American War the Brazos Island Supply Depot was the encampment for thousands of Union Soldiers waiting for assignment to other locations. It is assumed that these men were the laborers that were used to modify the survey markers at that location. Fortunately for history not all of the old markers were totally destroyed. Both the old defaced markers, the old intact markers, and the new markers placed by General Taylor, are all visible to the trained eye.

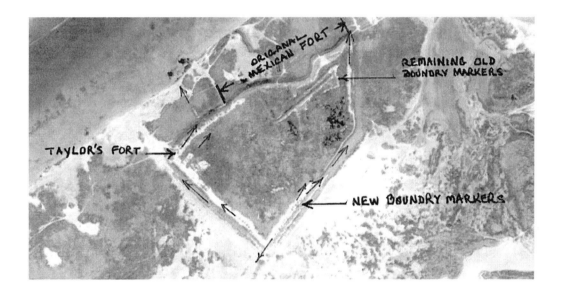

The Brazos Santiago Supply Depot

The above diagram shows a view of the Brazos Santiago Supply Depot from the air. The Triangle and liner mounds in the center of the barricade are the only remnants of the original markers within the fort. The new markers, constructed by General Taylor were incorporated into the walls of the fort which he completed. The Depot was constructed in two stages. The entire barricade, except for the area marked as the "Mexican Barricade" (See photo.), was constructed by General Taylor Circa 1848. The dots that can be seen on the top of the barricade, and the walls themselves, were designed to designate the new boundaries of what would become the United States. Evidently the earlier markings inside the fort went unnoticed, or General Taylor may have had a soft spot for history. Southeast of the Depot are where the earlier markers, designating Mesoamerica as part of the earlier land claim, were constructed. It was these geoglyphs that were destroyed in order to separate any connection between North America and Central America.

Hundreds of geoglyphs have been located within the United States which also confirms the pre-Columbian, pre-Cortes and post-Cortes boundaries of the North American Land Claim.

By whatever name you wish to call them, there is ample evidence, from many disciplines, which confirm that there were Europeans in the Americas long before current history will admit.

Closing Comment

There is currently much discussion over persons working, and making scientific discoveries outside of their academic field. This trend is inevitable as more scientific tools become available to intelligent people with curious minds. You would not expect a person with a Doctorate in their field to make many discoveries if they never enter a laboratory or venture into the field.

Conversely, you might expect an intelligent individual that has tools available and who is curious enough to venture into the unknown, and investigate something that is interesting to that person, to discover and collect information that has previously been unknown.

With the pace at which science is progressing we can no longer judge discoveries based on the field in which the person is schooled. As most learned persons will agree, real knowledge is gained after you leave the academic arena anyway.

To that end, I leave you with an excerpt from the works of the Dutch author Jan-Anton van Hoek - 1982

***

No wisdom is in him who is not free within himself, because he is a thoughtless slave of others, who think in his place or at least pretend.

No wisdom is in him also when he is deaf and blind, who believes what others see and hear in his place or pretend to do so.

No wisdom is in him neither who is frivolous to the all, because he is a spiritual fool, who leaves his responsibility to others, who pretend to fulfill the cosmic plights in his place.

The path that is open is not the one of the least resistance. In stead of other thoughts, enlightened or not, one has to think for oneself. Instead of echoing other's people's sentences, one shall have to learn to speak from oneself. But above all: instead of going to promised lands of eternity as if being part of a traveling companionship, one shall have to oneself find the answers to cosmic questions, and to find the spark in order to alight the innate eternal Light. The era of belief is totally over; the era of Cosmic Knowing has started.

Jan-Anton van Hoek - 1982

END CHAPTER

Juan de la Cosa 1450-1610

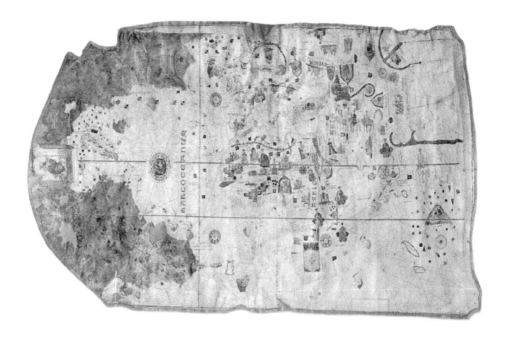

Original Colored Juan de la Cosa Map

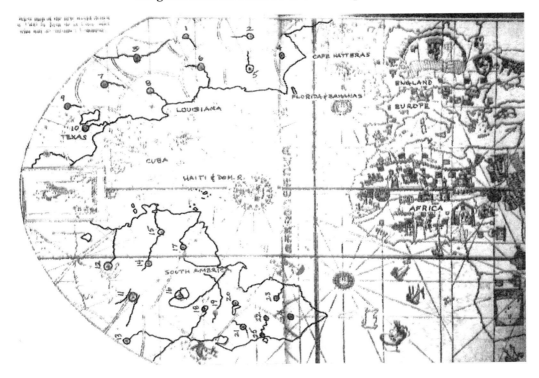

Black & White Map with River Geoglyphs Numbered

1. Seneca River, Phoenix, NY USA

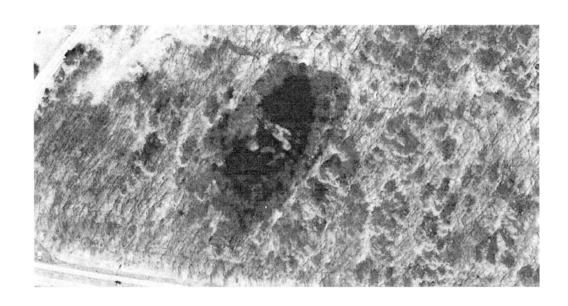

2. Delaware River, All-Seeing Eye (Lake), Port Jarvis, NY USA

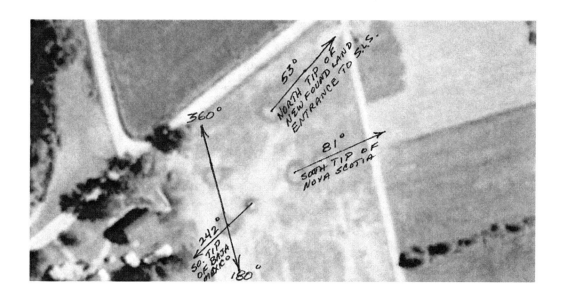

3. Tonawanda River, Lockport, NY USA

4. Urbanized Geoglyphs, Raleigh, NC USA

5. Urbanized Geoglyphs, Atlanta, GA USA

6. Apalachicola River, Wewahitchka, FL USA

7. Ohio River, "Cairo", IL USA

8. Mississippi River, Alcorn MS USA

275

9. Red River, Yarnaby, OK USA

10. Sabine River, South Toledo Bend, TX USA

**11. The Great Circle (22 miles across) Montero, Bolivia
(Showcased in the paper on Caral, Peru)**

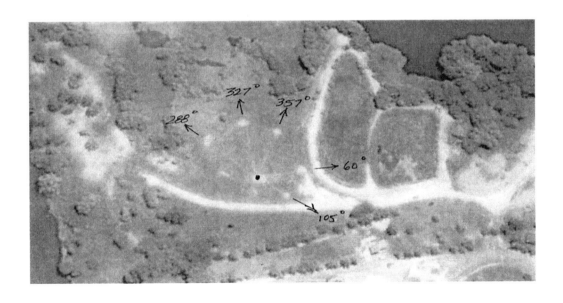

12. Magdalena River, Barranca Bermeja, Colombia

13. Urbanized Geoglyph, Majes River, Pampacolca, Peru

14. Oronoco River, Cambalache, Brazil

15. Urbanized Geoglyph, Tigre River, Tucupita, Venezuela

16. Pilotas River Lake Glyph, Marcelino Ramos, Brazil

17a. Canals on the Xangu River, Brazil

17b. Dot Glyphs on the Xangu River, Brazil

18. Urbanized Geoglyph, Copiapo River, Copiapo, Chile

19. Parana River, Rosario, Argentina

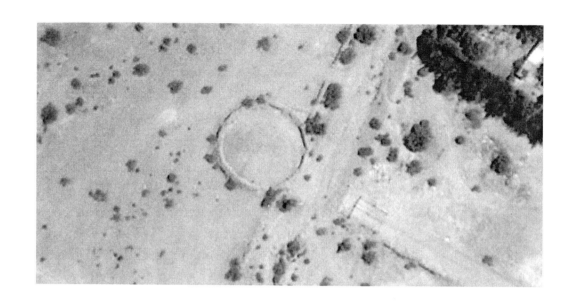

20. Elqui River, Vicuna Chile

21. Elqui River Entrance, La Serena, Chile

22. Bio-Bio River, Lija Falls, Chile

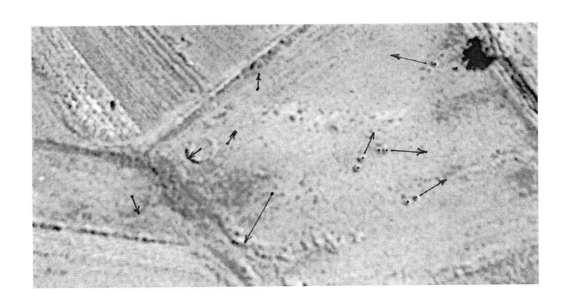

23. Chubut River, Gaiman, Argentina

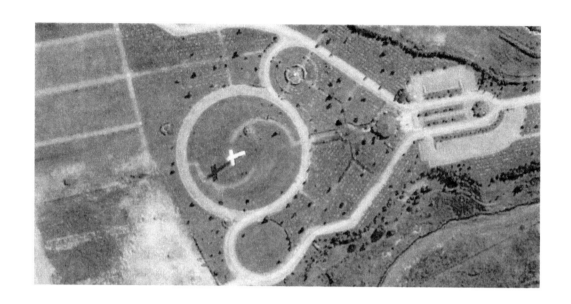

24. Straits of Magellan, Punta Arenas, Chile

25. Bio-Bio River, Haulpen, Chile

END OF APPENDIX A

DATING THE NEWPORT TOWER

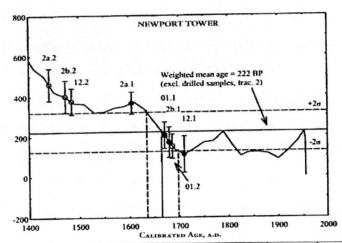

Position	Height above ground (cm)	Sample Depth (cm)	Sample No.	Lab. No. AAR	Fraction of total sample (%)	Carbonate concentration (%)	¹⁴C Age (BP)	δ¹³C (‰) PDB
TOWER:								
Flue above fireplace	550	Surface	X.1	1284.1	45	42	205±65	-12.3
			X.2	1284.2	55		190±60	-11.5
Pillar 7	110	7-12	2a.1	1352.1	20	22	365±55	-13.9
			2a.2	1352.2	80		460±80	-9.4
			2b.1	1352.3	50	17	170±75	-10.7
			2b.2	1352.4	50		400±80	-9.7
			3a.1	1504.1	83	2.0	No meas.	-10.8
			3a.2	1504.2	17		No meas.	
			3b.1	1504.3	40	1.3	No meas.	-11.3
			3b.2	1504.4	60		No meas.	-10.4
Fireplace	420	16-26W	1.1	1353.1	57	5.8	(-110±70)*	-13*
			1.2	1353.2	43		(190±70)*	-11.6
Pillar 6	20	10-25	12.1	1286.1	37	53	110±90	-13.4
			12.2	1286.2	63		375±65	-9.7
Pillar 8	250	Plaster	Bulk (conv.)	Hel-4181			290±110	-6.4
Excavated 1949			Ox bone	1280			25±60	-19.7
WANTON-LYMAN-HAZARD HOUSE:								
Basement	30	Surface	H 13.1	1287.1	52	70	80±100	-16.3
			H 13.2	1287.2	48		160±60	-13.3
* Excluded due to low carbonate content								

FIGURES 3 AND 4. HEINEMEIER AND JUNGNER CALIBRATION CURVES AND DATA TABLE.

Presented Above is The Heinemeier and Junger Report

Since 1996 when the team of Heinemeier and Junger performed carbon dating, using samples from the Newport Tower, their data has been considered flawed by some researchers. However, it is this researcher's opinion that neither their data nor their techniques were flawed. The outcome of the Heinemeier and Junger report was confusing because it developed not one, but two, closely grouped sets of data. Rob Carter summed it up when he wrote: "Other researchers working on this technique for dating stone structures in South America report success at dating pre-Columbian mortared walls. There were no serious inconsistencies between the carbon dates and other corroborating evidence. What made their work [Heinemeier and Junger] different?" It is this writer's opinion that the results were not different but led us to overlook the obvious. There are two camps of thought on the date of the Newport Tower. First there are the Templar enthusiasts who contend that the tower was constructed in the 15th Century. Second there are the Colonist Enthusiasts that claim that the tower was constructed in the 17th Century. I believe they are both correct. Is it not possible that the tower was built in the 15th Century, partially destroyed, and then rebuilt from the remains in the 17th Century? All signs point in that direction. This line of reasoning is especially compelling when it is considered that the Kensington Runestone, by necessity, was updated sometime after 1559.

1. The Heinemeier and Junger report shows two close groupings, one in the 15th Century and the other in the 17th Century.

2. The H & J Report contains so much data that a very important fact has been overlooked.

Their data is not arbitrary because each of the three samples that were used in their graph consistently contained both a 15th Century date and a 17th Century date. (The researchers were careful not to include samples which were flawed by low carbon content or from a possibly contaminated surface source.)

This can only lead a reasonable person to one logical conclusion. The tower was built in approximately 1463, the average of the three 15th Century dates presented in the data, and then rebuilt in approximately 1663, the average of the 17th Century data, using material from the old structure. Curiously, the average dates of construction are exactly 200 years apart. One carbon date of construction is prior to the North American Territory Change in 1519 and one carbon date is after the North American Territory Change that begins in 1519 with the invasion of Mexico by Hernando Cortes of Spain. (Explained in the Chapter "Hernando Cortez, The Game Changer".)

Sample.....................Date

2a1..........................1610
2a2..........................1440

2b1..........................1670
2b2..........................1470

12-1.........................1710
12-2.........................1480

END OF APPENDIX B

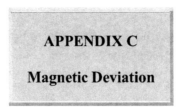

Magnetic Deviation and It's Affect on Navigating a Compass Heading

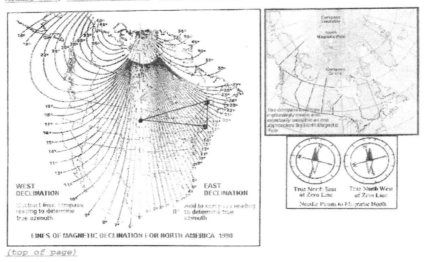

GEOMAGNETIC MAPS (dish size list or tuning page)
(to Western Hemisphere, Eastern Hemisphere, Footprints by Dish Size)

The most important geomagnetic fact to remember, the earth's magnetic field is neither uniform, stationary, nor perfectly aligned with the planet's poles. True north can be determined with a compass reading plus/minus (as appropriate) the location's magnetic deviation. Magnetic deviation (also called magnetic declination, magnetic variation, or compass variation) is the angle between the north compass (magnetic) heading and the heading to true (geographic) north. For absolute accuracy, you can call your local airport control tower to find the magnetic correction value for your area; this value can also be found on local maps though many maps ommit this value. The following maps are also called isogonic maps. North America, South America, Europe, Middle East, Orient/New Guinea, Australia/New Zealand, Global

WEST DECLINATION
Subtract from compass reading to determine true azimuth

EAST DECLINATION
Add to compass reading to determine true azimuth

LINES OF MAGNETIC DECLINATION FOR NORTH AMERICA 1990

(top of page)

Source: http://www.geo-orbit.org

Magnetic Deviation Chart for North America

The preceding chart, which depicts the North American Continent, shows the amount of Magnetic Deviation at any given point in the United States. On that chart you will notice that the Newport Triangle has been overlaid in its proper position. Notice that the Newport Triangle progresses from 5 degrees West deviation to 15 degrees East deviation, passing through the 0 degree line of deviation. That means that while progressing from the West side of the triangle to the East side you will pick up a 20 degree error. That error is demonstrated on the diagram that follows.

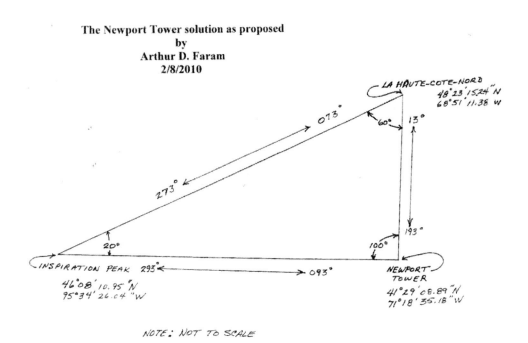

The Newport Triangle

Notice that the magnetic headings, obtained from the point of origination, from East to West and from West to East are exactly 20 degrees off from what they should be. The opposite heading on any true course should be exactly 180 degrees from each other. These magnetic headings are 20 degrees off as the result of the magnetic deviation along that line. That deviation does not exist in a true course plotted by celestial navigation or

GPS. How the ancient mariners did it is a mystery, but their calculations are correct anywhere from directly on target to being only a few hundred feet off, sometimes on courses extending over thousands of miles.

END OF APPENDIX C

Sources

The Faram Family History - As passed down by the Faram family.

The History and Future of Narragansett Bay - by Capers Jones (Mar 1, 2006)

Ancient Gods Speak - The: A Guide to Egyptian Religion by Redford, Donald B. 2002 Oxford University Press ISBN 0-19-515401-0

Atlas of Ancient Egypt - by Baines, John; Malek, Jaromir 1980 Les Livres De France Egyptian Religion Morenz, Siegfried 1973 Cornell University Press ISBN 0-8014-8029-9

Gods of the Egyptians - The (Studies in Egyptian Mythology) by Budge, E. A. Wallis 1969 Dover Publications, Inc. ISBN 486-22056-7

History of Ancient Egypt - by A. Grimal, Nicolas 1988 Blackwell Oxford History of Ancient Egypt, The Shaw, Ian 2000 Oxford University Press ISBN 0-19-815034-2

Oxford Illustrated History of Christianity - by McManners, John 1992 Oxford University Press ISBN 0-19-285259-0

The God Amun and Amun-Re - Article by Taylor Ray Ellison

Valley of the Kings - by Weeks, Kent R. 2001 Friedman/Fairfax ISBN 1-5866-3295-7

Archaeological Site in Peru Is Called Oldest City in Americas - by Henry Fountain, "The New York Times, April 27, 2001.

"Radio Carbon Dating in America's oldest city could mean adjusting history" - by Kevin Hall and Seth Bernstein, (Knight Ridder Newspapers) April 26, 2001.

"Postcards From The Amazon: Massive clues of the Amazon area's past" - J. Hoelle,San Angelo Standard Times, Posted July 31, 2010,

The Late Preceramic and Initial Period. In Peruvian Prehistory - by R. Pineda, (Richard W. Keatinge, Ed., Cambridge Univ. Press. 1988.)

The Hanseatic League at War - by Alex Graham-Heggie. (2009)

Amphibious Warfare in the Baltic - by Matthew Bennett. (1929)

The German Hansa - by Phillippe Dollinger. (1970)

Ships, Guns and Bibles in the North Sea and Baltic States - by David Ditchburn. (2000)

A Brief History of Edinburgh Scotland - by Tim Lambert.

The Scots in Germany - by Th A. Fischer (1902)

Relations Between England and Scotland - by Robert S. Rait (2007)

Saxo, Gesta Danorum - ed. Holder (Strassburg, 1886), books xvi.

Steenstrup, Danmarks Riges Historie - Oldtiden og den ldre Middelalder, pp. 570-735 (Copenhagen, 1897-1905).

Absalon's Testamentum, in Migne - Patrologia Latina 209,18.

Debrett's Kings and Queens of Great Britain - by Williamson, David

The Life of King Alfred - by Asser, Bishop of Sherborne,

Danelaw - by Adrienne Warber, 2009

Y - DNA: Paternal - David K. Faux

Aspects of Maritime Scandinavia AD 200- 1200 - Proceedings of the Nordic Seminar on Maritime Aspects of Archaeology, Roskidle, 13th-15th March, 1989, 1991

Trading Ships in Egil's Saga, The Sagas of Icelanders: - A Selection, preface by Jane Smiley, introduction by Robert Kellogg, 2000

The Huns in battle with the Alans - by Johann Nepomuk Geiger, 1873.

Loot and Land - by Dr. Anna Ritchie, Last updated 2009-11-05

'Did Jesus Come To Britain? - by Glyn Lewis' tome 2008

Strange Footprints on the Land - by Irwin, Constance; Harper&Row, New York, 1980; ISBN 0-06-022772-9

"The place of Greenland in medieval Icelandic saga narrative" - by Grove, Jonathan. 2009. in Norse Greenland: Selected Papers of the Hvalsey Conference 2008, Journal of the North Atlantic Special Volume 2, 30-51

"Norse voyages in the tenth and following centuries" - by Anderson, Rasmus B.; John Bruno Hare, ed., February 18th, 2004 (1906). The Norse Discovery of America. http://www.sacred-texts.com/neu/nda/nda27.htm. Retrieved 2008-08-27. "He remained there making explorations for three years and decided to found a colony there."

"Discovery and colonization of Greenland" - by Reeves, Arthur Middleton and Rasmus B. Anderson (1906). Saga of Erik the Red. http://www.sacred-texts.com/neu/nda/nda18.htm. Retrieved 2008-08-27.

The Seafarers: The Vikings - by Wernick, Robert; (1979), 176 pages, Time-Life Books, Alexandria, Virginia: ISBN 0-8094-2709-5.

Eric; The Norsemen(1965) - by Oxenstierna,320 pages, New York Graphic Soc.: ISBN 1-122-21631-9

The Vinland Sagas. - by Magnusson, Magnus; Palsson, Hermann (1965). Penguin Books. ISBN 9780140441543

Collapse: How Societies Choose to Fail or Succeed - by Diamond, Jared:

"Markland and Helluland" - Smithsonian National Museum of Natural History. pp. Archeology page and following.

http://www.mnh.si.edu/vikings/voyage/subset/markland/archeo.html.

The Norse discoverers of America, the Wineland sagas. - by Gathorne-Hardy, Geoffrey Malcolm (1920). Oxford: Clarendon press. http://www.archive.org/details/norsediscoverers00gathrich. Retrieved 2009-02-25.

Monarchs of the Nile - by Aidan Dodson, 1995

Journal of Anthropological Archaeology - 17,97-123 by Fred Wendorf and Romuald Schild (1998)

History of the Portuguese Discovery Monument Arthur Raposo's Dream - by Manuel Luciano da Silva, M. D.

The Portuguese Discoveries Monument at Brenton Point State Park, RI. - by Manuel Luciano da Silva, M. D.

1421, The Year China Discovered America - by Gaven Menzies, Transworld Publishers, UK 2002

The Ancient Mounds of Poverty Point - by Gibson, Jon L. (2000).Place of Rings. Gainesville, Florida: University Press of Florida.

The Moundbuilders: Ancient Peoples of Eastern North America - by Milner, George R. (2004).London: Thames & Hudson Ltd.

After the Ice - by Steven Mithen: Harvard University Press, Cambridge MA, 2004, ISBN 0-674-01570-3. Pp. 65 - 69, 89 - 90.

Archaeology - Theories, Methods and Practices. - by C. Renfrew and P. Bahn,(Thames and Hudson, 2004), Fourth Edition

Encyclopedia of Archaeology - by K. Hirst, Academic Press, Univ. of Missouri, Columbia, Sept. 2007, ISBN 13: 978-0-12-548030-7

Dating Caral, a preceramic site in the Supe Valley on the central coast of Peru, - by Dr. Ruth Shady Solis, Dr. Jonathan Haas, Dr. Winifred Creamer, Sci. Jour., 723-726., 27 April 2001, [DOI:10.1126/science.1059519]

"Caral - Cradle of American Civilization", January 2007, - by I. Nazarova, Peru , January, 2007., (available online at http://www.tiwy.com/pais/peru/caral/eng.phtml)

"The Tangut Royal Tombs near Yinchuan" - by Steinhardt, Nancy Shatzman (1993). Muqarnas (Brill Publishers) 10: 369 381. doi:10.2307/1523201.

The Secret Archives of the Vatican. - by Ambrosini, Lucy with Mary Willis. Little, Brown & Co., Boston, 1969.

The True Story of How America Got Its Name. - by Broome, Rodney.MJF Books, New York, 2001.

A Memoir of Sebastian Cabot. - by Biddle, Richard. Philadelphia, 1831. Reprinted in 1915.

History of the Indies. - by Casas, Bartolom de las.Harper & Row, New York, 1971,

The Discovery of North America. - by Harrisse, Henry. N. Israel, Amsterdam, 1961.

The Diplomatic History of America: - by Harrisse, Henry. Its First Chapter (1452-1494). B. F. Stephens Pub. London, 1897.

Cabot to Cartier. - by Hoffman, Bernard G. University of Toronto Press, 1961.

The House of Medici, Its Rise and Fall. - by Hibbert, Christopher. William Morrow, New York, 1975.

The Life and Voyages of Americus Vespucius. - by Lester, Edwards C. New Amsterdam Book Co., New York 1903.

The European Discovery of America. - by Morison, Samuel Eliot. in 2 volumes, Oxford University Press, 1974.

Admiral of the Ocean Sea, A Life of Christopher Columbus. - by Morison, Samuel Eliot. Little, Brown & Co., Boston, 1942.

Coleccion de los viages y descubriementos. - by Navarrete, Martin Fernandez de,5 volumes, Madrid, 1829.

Amerigo Vespucci Pilot Major. - by Pohl, Frederick J. Octogon Books, New York, 1966.

England and the Discovery of America. - by Quinn, David Beers. Alfred A. Knopf, New York, 1974.

The Columbus Myth, Did Men of Bristol Reach America Before Columbus? - by Wilson, Ian. Simon & Schuster, London, 1991.

John Cabot & the Matthew. - by Wilson, Ian. Redcliffe Press, Bristol, England, 1996.

The Voyages of the Cabots & The English Discovery of North America. - by Williamson, James, A. Argonaut Press, London, 1929.

The Columbus Myth Exposed at Last - by Kilkenny, Niall 2007

The Secret Destiny of America - by Manly P. Hall (1944)

Discovering the Mysteries of Ancient America: Lost History And Legends, Unearthed And Explored - by Frank Joseph, David Hatcher Childress, Zecharia Sitchin, and Wayne May (Jan 30, 2006)

The History and Future of Narragansett Bay - by Capers Jones (Mar 1, 2006)

History's Mysteries: People, Places and Oddities Lost in the Sands of Time - by Brian Haughton (Apr 20, 2010)

Ancient Footprints - by Gary R. Varner (Feb 14, 2010)

Atlantic Crossings Before Columbus - by Frederick Pohl (Mar 15, 2007)

Topographic survey map of the City of Newport, Rhode Island by Fenton G. Geys Associates - Sheet #51 - Office of City Engineer, Newport, Rhode Island.

Stonehenge Monolith, Salisbury, U.K. - Wikipedia, Keyword: Stonehenge.

Gulfo de Cintra Glyphs, Western Sahara, Africa - Google Earth Viewpoint 23 01 32.66 N 16 07 04.64 W

Genteel Rhetoric: Writing High Culture in Nineteenth-Century Boston. - Broaddus, Dorothy C.,Columbia, South Carolina: University of South Carolina, 1999

The Moral Argument Against Calvinism. - Channing, William Ellery. Pages 39-59 in Unitarian Christianity and Other Essays . Edited by Irving H. Bartlett. Indianapolis: Bobbs-Merrill; 1957 [1820]. Cited in Finlan, Stephen. Jesus in Atonement Theories. In The Blackwell Companion to Jesus. Edited by Delbert Burkett. London: Blackwell; 2010

The Hooked X: Key to the Secret History of North America - by Scott F. Wolter (Aug 3, 2009)

Memoir of William Ellery Channing: - with extracts from his correspondence, Volume 2 p416

Website References:

"Satellite Detects Ruins of Ancient Civilization in Brazil, Finds Giant Geoglyphs." - http://beforeitsnews.com/story/81/992/Satellite_Detects_Ruins_of_Ancient_Civilization_in_Brazil,_Finds_Giant_Geoglyphs.html)

Understanding Chavin and the Origins of Andean Civilization - http://www.jqjacobs.net/andes/chavin.html

Andean Archaeology Papers - http://andean.kulture.org/owen/index.html

Archaeology Research in Peru - http://bruceowen.com/research/researchperu.htm

Galician Geneology - http://www.rollintl.com/roll/galicia.htm

http://www.forvo.com/search/faram/en/

Your Source of Knowledge on Celts - http://www.essortment.com/all/celtichistorya_rmog.htm

Ancient Celtic Clans, - http://www.celticclans.org/history.html

The Spindlers on Celts - http://www.en.wikipedia.org/wiki/Galatia

Ancient History of the Celts - http://www.celts.org.uk/

Ancient History of the Cities of the World - http://www.localhistories.org

Avignon - http://www.en.wikipedia.org/wiki/Avignon

The Celts - http://www.en.wikipedia.org/wiki/Celts

Templers Treasure - http://www.templartreasure.com

World Geography - http://www.earth.google.com

The Complete Archaeology Web - http://www.comp-

archaeology.org/WendorfSAA98.html
Symbols - http://www.crossroad.to/Books/symbols1.html
The Pentagram -
http://www.mediade.si/media/symbolic.meaning.of.the.pentagram.extract.pdf
Dictionary of Symbols - http://www.symboldictionary.net
The Mariner's Museum - http://www.marinersmuseum.org/
Magnetic Deviation - http://www.geo-orbit.org
Christopher Columbus - http://www.causamerita.com/enigmas.htm
History of the Newport Tower -
http://www.dightonrock.com/portuguese_tower_of_newport.htm
The Newport Tower Mystery Solved - http://www.thenewporttower.com
The Kensington Runestone Mystery Solved -
http://www.thekensingtonrunestone.com
Spirituality and Religion - http://www.beliefnet.com
History of Scotland -
http://www.electricscotland.com/webclans/stoz/sinclai2.html
Preservation of History - http://www.nps.gov
Science News- http://sciencev1.orf.at/science/news/282
Portuguese History - www.golisbon.com/culture/history.html
Some information released under the GNU Free Documentation License -
http://www.gnu.org/copyleft/fdl.html

Further Reading:

Online Keywords: Geoglyphs, Archaeology, Amazon Geoglyphs, Peruvian Geoglyphs, Caral Peru, Newport Tower, Celts, Kensington Runestone, Runestones in America, Mississippian Tribes, Egyptian Pyramids, Pyramids of Mexico, Xian Pyramids, Turkish Pyramids, Vikings in America.

END

CPSIA information can be obtained at www.ICGtesting.com
Printed in the USA
LVOW122145190712

290778LV00016B/146/P